# Divine Purpose

## Find the Passion Within

### Cynthia Yoder

## Open Door Publications, LLC

Divine Purpose
Find the Passion Within

Published by
Open Door Publications
27 Carla Way
Lawrenceville, NJ 08648
www.OpenDoorPublications.com


Cover Artwork: detail of the sculpture "Clyde's Emerson" by artist Jerry
Wennstrom
www.HandsofAlchemy.com


Cover Design by
Sandy Gans
www.SandyToesCreative.com


ISBN: 9780982891827

For Jonathan and Gabe

# Acknowledgements

This was my favorite page to write, as it is an example of how carrying out our purpose emerges from the web of community, colleagues, friends and family that surrounds us every day.

First of all, this book would not be in the world at all were it not for Karen Miller, who urged me to collect my writings and publish them. Her unique combination of patience and drive, as well as encouragement to push the boundaries of my own writing, provided the perfect set of conditions for the writing of *Divine Purpose.* Thank you, Karen, for all that you have done—from holding the vision all the way down to page design!

Also, I am so grateful to friend and artist Jerry Wennstrom for allowing us to use a detail of his sculpture, *Clyde's Emerson,* for the cover art. Jerry's own journey to understand his purpose is so inspiring that I urge you to read his memoir that chronicles his journey. I've included a note about him at the end of this book. Thank you, Jerry! And thank you, Sandra Gans for your creativity in putting together a knock-out book cover design.

I thank my mentor Al Dumapit for your steady and skillful guidance in helping me refine and live out my own purpose. Thank you also to business coach Patrick Dominguez for your transformative insights, guidance and vision. I remember wisdom teacher David La Chapelle, with whom I studied and apprenticed for six years. Though he is no longer here in body, his spirit and his teachings breathe through everything I have written here.

This book has drawn on the well of David's teachings, study of my own and others' process of discovery, as well as insights born of the many keen and pointed questions asked by clients. I thank these deep souls for the sincerity and thoroughness of your questions.

I also thank all of my friends and family, whose friendship and support of my work is more valuable than I can articulate. I thank these lovely beings especially who contributed to various aspects of the physical and conceptual material that make up this book: Jacqueline Knox, Patricia Weimer, Dani Antman, Yvonna Leutzinger, and my sister Juanita Yoder.

I thank my parents for being loving and supportive role models of living with purpose and peace. Finally, I thank Jonathan, my husband, for being a pillar of support and love, and our son Gabe for your sweet enthusiasm as I've put together this book.

# Table of Contents

# Seeking

Why do I look for you,
when you are my eyes?
Why do I pray to you,
when you are my voice?
Why do I long for you, all the while
you are my breathing in and my breathing out?

Oh Beloved. Keep me awake
in this temple.
Let the ways of your Heart
be known within my own.
Let my feet mark your footsteps.
Let my hands be your blessing.

Grace is seated at my doorstep.
I open the door to my heart,
and she is there, offering
a drink from the fountain
of Eternal Compassion.

I call, *Oh Beloved*, and
I hear you answer the same.

# Part One

# Creating Conditions for Purpose

# 1: The Unfolding of Purpose

The path toward understanding purpose is to bring awareness to what makes you feel alive and to share that aliveness with others. You are continually unfolding your purpose as you live. From the moment you were born, you were born *on purpose*. When you bring awareness to this purpose, you can embrace your life in a new way and experience how this purpose has formed your life and continues to form it.

There are fundamental ways to describe purpose, such as "to love," or "to be," or "to become." Yet our personal expression of purpose in the world, through our work and relationships, may require some further soul searching. It is the intention of this book to give you tools for that search, so that you can live in the unfolding of this purpose with awareness and grace.

I first realized the power of purpose only a few years ago, when I was visiting a dear teacher who was dying of cancer. I had been studying and apprenticing with spiritual teacher David La Chapelle for six years, and it was difficult to see him slipping away. Yet at the foot of such loss, the lens through which one sees life shifts dramatically. As I sat by a mountain stream in his hometown in Colorado, I watched the power of the water as it washed over the rocks in its course down the mountain, noticing how nothing stood in the path of this immense force.

Studying with David and then serving him through his illness created a powerful context for my life that I had never before experienced. In that moment by the stream, I could see that having a context for your life brings guidance to all that you do in the same way that the banks of a river guide its flow. Where rocks and branches may otherwise create several meandering brooks with no direction, a river held within banks will run powerfully over and around these potential blockages. All of the river's energy is used in carrying out its mission of flowing toward the sea.

Purpose can provide context for our lives like this, so that all of our choices and aspirations can move in one clear and intentional direction. Purpose can also provide momentum, so that when we experience blockages – the rocks and branches of life—we continue on our course despite these obstacles. We open our hearts to experience the flow of grace in our lives.

# Contemplation

Write out your intentions for how you will use this book to explore purpose. Will you journal weekly? Or will you take a few days, weeks or months and work through the contemplations? Create an intentional relationship with the purpose exploration that you are doing. Write down what you would like to get out of working through these pages. Do you want to understand your nature and expression more thoroughly? Do you want to discover what you are here to do? Is it knowing that *and* applying that to a new project or job? Do you want support for a purpose you already know is yours to do? Writing this down is your commitment to yourself to allow yourself to transform through the work and reflection that you do. This kind of commitment will help you deal with resistance if it arises.

# Reflections and Wonderings

# 2: Why Purpose Matters

We come into this life without a map, and yet in the deepest part of our being, there is an unfolding of our purpose that shows us the way.

If not answered satisfactorily, the universal question of "why am I here?" can lead to feelings of hopelessness and despair. In my own journey, I have experienced periods of feeling lost in the dark before understanding my purpose and how to give that purpose expression in the world. My first book, *Crazy Quilt: Pieces of a Mennonite Life,* is a chronicle of seeking this deeper fulfillment and confronting the inner demons that can arise along the way!

Purpose is like an anchor for our awareness. We will still have everyday struggles and challenges and moments of feeling lost. But purpose provides a deeper understanding that can direct and inspire our steps every day.

That doesn't mean that our purpose unfolds all at once. It doesn't. I regularly meet with people who are living out their purpose fully but who want feedback on next steps. Sometimes those next steps aren't clear. But what does remain clear is an understanding or vision that holds the process.

Right now, your purpose may be to discover your purpose! Gautama Buddha said, "Your work is to discover your work and then with all your heart to give yourself to it."

Your purpose is a passionate calling, a drawing outward of who you are so that the world can benefit from this expression. We are bombarded in our culture with messages about how our lives should look on the outside. But often those messages run counter to the deeper promptings of our heart and soul. This conflict makes it very hard to listen to those inner messages.

Knowing that we can attain a deeper vision for our lives can bring the motivation needed to overcome these inner conflicts. When we give attention to something with all of our heart, we can see that our gifts and our values matter, and that they truly can make a difference in the world.

You are living your purpose today, in this very moment. You cannot be alive without living your purpose out. You may not be aware of what it is, but you are living it. Everything you do matters. When you breathe, you participate in the breath of life. When you have lunch with a friend, you increase the expression of love in the world. When you help create understanding of someone's financial picture, you increase the feeling of being held in the world.

Purpose can be grand and large and visionary, and it can be very small and subtle and simple. Purpose is an anchor for an awareness of the contribution we make every day of our lives.

# Contemplation

Reflect on how living with a sense of purpose would affect your life and how this might serve those around you. Contemplate how your living and acting from a place of purpose would impact your relationships, your work, your health and well-being and your greater world.

Write down each area and describe what these areas are like now and how being on purpose will bring positive change to these areas.

Write down your commitment to yourself to bring this positive change into reality.

# Reflections and Wonderings

# 3: Divine Purpose

In putting language to the mysterious, ineffable Presence that has been described and named throughout history in so many ways, there is a risk in making this Presence feel smaller, more contained. However, for the sake of being able to say anything at all about how this Presence relates to our lives and purpose, I use the words "Divine," "Beloved" and "Presence" interchangeably throughout this book, as well as a few other descriptions. You will have your own words for this Presence!

Our highest purpose is an unfolding of this Divine Presence through us. Though we do the searching, and we carry out the work, we follow the promptings of the heart that are the very voice of the Beloved prompting us to come forward. In this unfolding, we become what St. Francis called "instruments of Thy peace."

Divine Purpose unfolds from activity that takes us to this place of union, this place of becoming a vessel. I'm not talking about prayer or worship here, though they may be your activities! I'm getting at whatever activity leads to this union through *your* actions in the world. For Mother Teresa, it was serving the poor with her own hands. For Harriet Tubman, it was guiding slaves to freedom in the North. For Martin Luther King, it was being a voice of liberation in a time of deep oppression.

As we search to understand our Divine Purpose, we search for guidance from that deepest prompting of the soul. This prompting is often called "intuition," yet there is a place where it becomes quite mystical, when this prompting gives us premonitions or a synchronous awareness of thoughts and events that the rational mind could not have generated.

In the mystical sides of many world religions, this awareness of the greater Presence within forms the basis for all correct action. When we go deep into the center of experience, we find God, and God is at the helm of our lives. A Sufi proverb touches on this: "I searched for God and found only myself. I searched for myself and found only God."

# Contemplation

Reflect back on your life to find one time in which you felt prompted to do something that felt unified with a greater Presence within. It may be helping out a friend who was in need or following an inner prompt to enter a certain course of study that inspired you. It may be taking on a project at work that was deeply fulfilling to you. Recall that experience vividly in your mind. How did you feel? What were you doing that evoked this inner experience? Write down this or any other experiences you had that brought you close to experiencing this union of the personal and transpersonal. This will give you some clues about your Divine Purpose.

# Reflections and Wonderings

# 4: The Web of Life Needs You

When we consider our purpose, it is often the case that we feel small and insignificant. We may wonder how following our purpose can make a difference in the world. This may be especially true at this time on our planet.

War, global weather change and 24-hour news broadcasts that bring the world's griefs to our doorstep can leave us feeling overwhelmed. It is a time in which following what moves us and fills us is more crucial than ever.

Each of us is part of an immense web of life, from the tiniest particles of matter to the distant stars. The Christian belief that we are the Body of Christ—we are one, connected, Divine body—is shared by other world religions as well. As a member of this greater Body, it is important that we do what we are here to do.

If you are meant to be the heart, and care for people with all your being, then you have no choice but to be that heart. If you are the feet, and bring stability through organizing or engineering the structures we experience daily, then you must be those feet!

If you are the hands and you love designing clothes to help people bring greater expression to their lives, then I'm jumping up and down to tell you that you must be the hands!

When we struggle against our own nature and purpose, it only causes unnecessary suffering and grief. I have experienced this myself and wrestled quite a bit with my own destiny. But when you do the inner work required to accept who you are and what you are being prompted to do, it creates a flow and sense of fullness in life that is transformational and worth every bit of effort.

The web of life needs people who are alive and willing to take risks and recreate themselves and try new things to create a world we all want to live in. It begins with each individual. It begins with you!

# Contemplation

Contemplate all of human life as one singular Body. What is your strength in this Body? What parts are you drawn to? Consider all of the jobs and hobbies that you have had so far. What were your strengths in carrying out your tasks? How do those strengths relate to how you might serve the whole Body of humanity?

The Dalai Lama and Ammachi (the "hugging saint") are two public servants who are having a global impact in following their purpose and whose humility and grace inspire millions of hearts. You can watch their demeanor on interviews or ceremonies on YouTube. Reflect on their essential love and delight in fulfilling their destiny and how this impacts the people they relate to directly and indirectly.

# Reflections and Wonderings

# 5: Honor the Process

It is important in considering your purpose that you don't judge your life. It is easy to feel "off track" if you have followed a path you feel is off-purpose. Truthfully, purpose is an unfolding. It unfolds from where you are, right now. It has been unfolding since you were born. Even if you feel completely lost, this is only a point of awareness that signals that you are ready to be found.

In my own experience, the darkest moments I've experienced occur just before a door opens, and new light and opportunities flood in. This is often true for others. The dark is simply a point of awareness. If you are depressed, and stuck in a long period of darkness, you may be more than willing to embrace the light but not see the way out. But it is important to keep faith that change will come.

I like to think of darkness as the bud of a rose. The bud will not say: "Shame on me for being in this dark place. I have lost my way. I am hopeless." The bud simply opens, when the conditions of light, soil and rain nurture its opening.

Honor the process. Honor your choices. If you proceed honoring the process itself, your purpose will unfold more gracefully. I recommend spending time doing a life review. In this review, which can be written or contemplative, ask yourself what you have learned. You may see that life has its own intelligence. Your path may twist and turn and have high peaks and lows, or it may feel flat. But if you are honest with yourself about what each peak or each valley or each flat plain has taught you, you will find how life has orchestrated itself on your soul's behalf.

When you seek your purpose in life, you are bringing the light of awareness to the process simply by your seeking. Nurturing conditions for your opening are crucial. This might include increasing your level of self-care. It may mean finding a friend or mentor to support you in the process. It may be finding a community of like minds, where you can feel like you have company on the path.

Given the right conditions, the bud of your soul will become a rose, fragrant and delicate and ready to share itself more completely.

# Contemplation

Buy yourself a rose this week. Contemplate the flower, its petals, its scent, its essence.

Now imagine the rose bush that produced this rose. Imagine how many years from seed to bush, how many years of needing tending and feeding and watering. And once a bud, how many moments between petals opening to create this singular, exquisite bloom.

Keep this rose nearby as you do a life review. What have you learned in the key experiences or key choices you have made? Write down the "soil" conditions you need to support your search for purpose. Here are some ideas:

Friends who listen well
Community
A mentor
Exercise
Meditation
Family time
Time alone

What is one thing you can do this week to invite one or more of these conditions into your life?

# Reflections and Wonderings

# 6: The Small Choices Matter

If you are looking for purpose and passion in your life, there is a good chance that you are looking for a major change. And while major change can be beneficial, the smallest choices that we make toward that larger change are most beneficial. Minor choices are not only important for shaping the reality we wake up to, but they are also shifts that create necessary movement.

And movement is everything. As my mother has said on more than one occasion, "God cannot steer a car if it is parked in a lot." Movement is your signal to yourself, Divine guidance and your world that you are ready for a shift.

Small steps, of course, can feel painfully small. However, when we are seeking purpose, each step has its own miniature purpose. Your miniature purpose right now may be simply to spend thirty minutes per day with this book working through its questions.

But there are other arenas that you can work on simultaneously to support a deeper sense of meaning and purpose in your life. If your work is less than satisfactory, see if you can take just a few minutes each day to reflect on what aspects of your work you are grateful for. Think of your colleagues, the building, the work, the impact your work has on others. There will most likely be something there that deserves gratitude, even if it is simply having money to keep a roof over your head.

Whatever arises in our lives challenges us to grow and change and become bigger beings than we were before. Spending some time in gratitude shapes our experience of our work and the people we relate with. If where you work feels less than ideal, bring in a fresh bouquet of flowers to shift the energy there or bring in a box of chocolates to share. If you are regularly surrounded by negative personalities, you can mix it up by introducing playful dynamics such as "strange hat day" or "bring your stuffed animal to work day." It is hard to stay locked in the negative in the face of playfulness.

Making small changes may seem obvious, but it is easy to miss. We may feel stuck in a web of habitual relating and think we need sweeping change, when small simple tweaks may help shift the dynamic we find ourselves in. It may at least provide some temporary relief as you explore other options.

All of our small choices create how we experience life as a whole. Although having a deeper vision for your life matters, what matters more are the choices that you make now, today, in this very moment. Life unfolds from where you are. So it is important to embrace where you are, who is around you and the body that you have been granted for carrying out your purpose.

As we make the seemingly minor choices that make up our day, we create the world we live in by these choices, and we set into motion the future that we are drawing to ourselves.

## Contemplation

Love someone today. Express gratitude for who this person is for you.

Love with your eyes, love with your smile. Love with a card. Love with a gift.

Loving others creates instant purpose. In the moment you share your heart with someone else, a doorway opens in the heart to a much larger Presence and purpose.

Write down a minor choice or a set of choices that you can make daily to invite purpose in your life.

Commit to doing these.

If you need self-love, then find a self-loving activity to immerse yourself in today.

# Reflections and Wonderings

# 7: You Are a Bright Vessel

Self-care is something that deserves a book all of its own, as it is a missing link for many people. I certainly have found it a challenge. Beneath the desire for living a purposeful, passionate life is a creaturely body needing reassurance that it is cared for and tended with love. When we become stressed by the various challenges of life, it is our creaturely body that reacts. We may breathe more shallowly; we may have stress signals in the heart or back or other areas.

It is very difficult for the higher functioning mind and spirit to embrace purpose if the very basic needs of the body are not being met. It is already difficult for our creaturely selves to reach outside our comfort zone. But if that creaturely self is feeling overworked, stressed emotionally, or just plain spent, the resistance to change will be that much greater.

Our creaturely body is very good at speaking to us about tending its needs. If a small "hello!" of an ache or pain is ignored, it will scream, "HELLO!" with a larger symptom. Listen to the conversation your body is trying to have with you. Once you fulfill your creaturely needs, you will be able to face change much more readily.

If we think of purpose as our lives in bloom in the world, our bodies might be the stems, supporting this unfolding. Any gardener will tell you that a wilted stem will not support a blooming, healthy flower. Either the bud will wither or the bloom will be only partial.

Self-care may be especially difficult for women, who early on may get the message that their role is to care for others. Self-care may feel selfish or simply unnecessary. However, the airlines have it right in this regard. If needing oxygen, first put the oxygen mask over your own nose and mouth, then put the mask on your child. Tending to your own needs first makes you more prepared and ready to tend the needs of others!

The Christian tradition teaches that the body is the house of the Spirit. It is your bright vessel, helping you carry out your purpose with vitality and enthusiasm! It is critical that you care for your body in a way that allows you to flourish as this sacred vessel.

# *Contemplation*

What are your favorite ways to tend to yourself? If you have none, then it's time to create some ways! Here are some suggestions:

Bathe with sea salts
Lying on the grass
Sitting on a comfortable chair with a good book
Sitting by a fire with a soft blanket
Playing sports
Eating nourishing food
Cooking or baking comfort foods
Having family or friends over for a meal or a movie

Here are five one-minute nourishing activities:

Bend over and hang like a ragdoll, then slowly straighten to standing
Take a breath into your belly, fill up the top of your lungs, holding for a moment, then release
Light a candle or use aromatherapy to please your senses
Think of a person you love, visualize this person in the place of your heart and express gratitude for them

What can you do today to nourish yourself?

# Reflections and Wonderings

# 8: Finding Space

On the journey toward purpose, it is important to have space for your inner world to reveal itself. In a world of instant access to communication, it is sometimes hard to find this space. Such spaciousness is more easily found on a snow day, or a vacation day, when life has slowed down and we can open our awareness to a deeper connection. But it can be found daily, too, with intention placed on finding ways to connect inward that are not based on doing or thinking but are rather based on simply being.

The natural world can help create this spaciousness. If you sit in your living room to reflect on purpose, the phone may ring, or you may hear that someone has sent you an email or text message. If you leave these devices and sit in the back yard, or go for a walk in the park, you will create space for yourself to reflect. This sounds obvious! But I meet people who have a hard time either disconnecting or simply taking the time to care for themselves in this way.

One of my favorite book titles as a college student was *A Room of One's Own.* I enjoyed Virginia Woolf's book, but the book title stuck with me long after I'd forgotten the particulars of the writing. It stayed with me as a kind of mantra, a vision, a reminder of some key to a magic doorway. Having space and time to be alone, to reflect, to simply *be*, without distraction, helps till the soil of your life, so that purpose and meaning can grow in an organic way. Everyone needs room to think or just be.

I lived in some very small spaces in my young adult life, but from the start, I created a space where I could work that was all my own. Even if it was a tiny writing desk in the living room, it was my desk, and all of my dreams, hopes and sorrows had a place to land there. Having a place, or an outdoor space that we go to, can provide just that extra little something we need to give attention to our inner life.

In some ways, we in the West have returned to the "constant contact" of village life, except now a lot of our contact is virtual. It may take extra effort to find that alone time, that empty space, where our dreams and thoughts can wander. It is an era in which I can see the wisdom of a Sabbath day. How essential it is for the soul to have time carved out to intentionally pause the hurried activity of the world. How necessary to have a time for reflection and approaching the holy ground within.

# Contemplation

Take stock of your week and carve out the space you need for contemplation and inner listening. If you are considering what to give up, consider how having a purpose will positively impact the other areas of your life. If you resist this idea, ask yourself why. Ask your resistance, *"Why?"*

Your inner listening can occur during many different activities. It can be while jogging as you focus on your steps to quiet your mind. It can be while listening to quieting music. It can be while sitting and watching the crackling of a fire. It can be on the train as you commute to work. It can be while journaling. Come up with a way that suits you best, and commit to this listening practice for fifteen minutes daily or at least once per week.

# Reflections and Wonderings

# 9: Mindful Action

The path toward purpose is truly a healing journey. Purpose unfolds from the inside out, so instead of looking outside ourselves for what will create meaning for us, we are asked to look within and follow the deeper promptings of our souls. As we look inward, we heal the places in ourselves that sought these answers from some external source.

Following inner promptings cannot happen when we move too fast through the hours and the day. One time-honored practice to help slow us down is practicing mindful action. In slowing down to pay close attention to what we are doing in the moment, our whole being can relax and open to the unfolding of our deeper purpose.

Once I took on a practice of baking bread for thirty days, a practice given to me by my spiritual teacher who suggested that I was moving too fast. Baking yeast bread—which required time to mix, time to knead, time to let rise, time to punch down and let rise again—required a level of patience that I did not have. I soon acquired it! And through the process, I began to understand how moving slowly requires us to be present in each moment, whether we are experiencing joy or suffering. Mindfulness requires that we experience the totality of the moment.

One of my favorite mindfulness practices is chanting a mantra while doing dishes, showering, or doing laundry. This focuses the mind in a way that erases random thought patterns and raises the awareness of the everyday sacred nature of these activities. Another is mindful eating. Mindful eating can be practiced by paying close attention to the sensory aspects of food – texture, color, aroma, taste, as well as chewing slowly and completely. You may even think of all of the people who helped get this food to your table, for example, from the grower to the driver to the grocer. In carrying out everyday activities mindfully, you focus the mind to support a deeper arising of purpose.

Life is full of suffering and discontentment as well as deep joy. In practicing being mindful and gentle with our actions, our suffering and our joy are held in loving hands and loving intention. Slowing down to mindfully participate in our daily activities helps give life an essential quality of being here and being present to each arising feeling and sensation. This itself generates meaning and purpose.

# Contemplation

It takes practice to bring one's attention fully to a task, to be fully present with it. Take stock of your daily tasks, especially those mundane tasks that you engage in after working hours. Whether it is cooking, stacking or washing dishes, folding laundry, eating a meal or taking out the garbage, select one task that you would like to practice doing mindfully. For one week, practice moving through this task with more mindfulness than usual. As you do this task, try these approaches:

> Pay attention to the pace of your steps or other movements.
> Pay attention to the pace of your breath.
> Offer gratitude for having the well-being and resources required to carry out the task.
> Add a prayer, song or a mantra that would help the task feel more meaningful.

Keep a record for yourself of what you practiced, to create accountability for yourself. Or mark your calendar so that you are reminded of what to practice.

# Reflections and Wonderings

# 10: Resistance to Your Path

We are all asked to be a light in the world, and how we embrace our own light is our unique path, based on our unique design and set of circumstances. What seems true for all of us is that when we shine our light we become hands and feet for a much larger light. The personal drops away, and the commonality of our experience truly blazes.

However, if you are like me or many of the people I know and work with, you may have deep resistance to stepping fully into your destiny. Resistance is not a bad thing. Resistance provides a workout for the mind and body to gain strength and resilience for the work ahead. When we meet our inner challenges, inner strength and resolve are called out of us. Our capacity grows.

However, resistance can also become a hindering block, keeping us from moving forward at all. You know you are stuck when you keep hearing the same inner prompting to do something, and yet you still don't do it. I've had periods of time when I've been seriously stuck. In these times, my physical body hurts, and my dreams become dark. These are indicators of blocked energy that is ready to move!

If we find ourselves stuck for long periods, we may manifest health issues, relationship difficulties or creative stagnation. There is a logjam in the system.

One of the best tools I know to deal with resistance is prayer and meditation. Prayer moves the realm of "doing" from the individual and places it at the feet of the larger Divine doing. This is an act of surrender that helps break through the energy of resistance. Similarly, meditation is an act of surrendering the mind to a greater awareness. Even if that awareness is the breath, we suspend personal will and thought momentarily for a deeper experience of awareness.

We are at a time on the planet when all souls are needed to help us evolve as a people and heal our hurting planet and communities. Each contribution matters, as each glowing light contributes to the illumination of the whole. It is a good time to ask whether you are working through your challenges and building capacity or whether you are seriously stuck and need to find a new approach so that you can address your challenges and move back into a more fluid way of being. Just the simple act of acknowledging where you are can create the necessary movement for your next unfolding.

## Contemplation

How do you express your light in the world?

In what way do you resist your own journey or your own promptings?

Are there things you feel prompted to do that you have not followed up on? Turn to the next page and see if you can tap into the voice of your own resistance. The voice that makes excuses, that doesn't want to do any of this. Write out all of the reasons you don't step into what you would like to step into.

Now pull back the lens and look at the writing as if from the perspective of a loving parent. What is real in those words? What is unreal and made up as a means of avoidance? Write a response from the perspective of a loving parent (imaginary or real) who is supporting your path. What would he or she have to say about all of this?

Watch for places of self-judgment and let them go. This is about naming the experience without judging it.

# Reflections and Wonderings

# 11: Embracing Suffering

Having a definite purpose can help us meet our challenges in a new way. No matter what our circumstances, all of us must trudge through the many trials life brings our way. A sense of purpose can give us the motivation to find our way to new light and new growth on the other side.

Seen one way, life is a place of purification, where all of our habitual and self-defeating tendencies are burned off, bit by bit, so that we can radiate out more of the love that is our true nature. In some spiritual traditions, it is taught that we are changed through life experience into the likeness of Infinite Love.

Through this lens, life is a refining fire, where circumstances arise to help us let go of our small, ego self and surrender to the more Pure Love that makes up our nature.

To take life's challenges as purification is to embrace suffering as life's deepest and truest teacher. Accepting suffering as part of the way of the Divine, we can bow to what it teaches us, embrace our hardships and become in that embrace a much fuller and wiser being.

This perspective is echoed in the Biblical *Book of Romans: We also rejoice in sufferings, knowing that suffering produces endurance; and endurance, character; and character, hope. And hope does not disappoint.*

Suffering, when embraced, purifies our nature and ultimately gives us hope. It is a paradox, as we are often taught by example to avoid suffering, but to avoid it is to miss the opportunity to embrace the fullness of our being.

As you seek to understand your purpose, suffering is one of life's greatest gifts. Suffering tears the veils away from your eyes, so that you can more fully understand yourself and life. Embracing your own suffering, you see more clearly the suffering nature of humanity. You see the many illusions that you and others create to avoid this suffering.

Embracing our true and most complex nature, our challenges become simpler because we see that they are opportunities to see life with clearer eyes and to experience life and its essence more completely.

# Contemplation

What are your challenges and points of suffering? How are your challenges highlighting old patterns, old ways of being, old forms, old beliefs and asking for something new?

What is the new impulse that wants to emerge? Take just one challenge you might be facing, whether it's a relationship, a financial situation, or a work issue. What is being asked of you? How is your essential nature being called forward?

When framed in this way, challenges are a blessing in disguise. Not that the challenges aren't sometimes very difficult, but when framed correctly, we can accept the simplicity of what is being asked. Take some time to look for the blessing. Make it a treasure hunt. And if you can't find it, ask a friend or a mentor to help you on the hunt. The treasure is always there.

# Reflections and Wonderings

# 12: Stillness and Surrender

In many spiritual traditions, stillness is a gateway to wisdom. Seated in stillness under a tree, the Buddha realized the interconnectedness of all things and experienced enlightenment. Jesus wandered the desert for forty days to confront temptation and to open the path to his compassionate teachings. St. Teresa of Avila spent long periods of time in prayer, leading to ecstatic union with the Divine as well as potent teachings and writings about the nature of this union.

The wisdom to understand our purpose in the world emerges from periods of stillness and deep listening apart from our daily activities.

Stillness can be very confronting to the sense of self and to the sense of having control over one's life. In the stillness of a moment, I am often alarmed at how much my mind jumps around as though dancing to its own tune. How is it that the mind seems to have a mind of its own? I cannot will the thoughts away. I must simply be with them. I must simply be with myself and my own chaos.

Stillness takes forgiveness. We have to forgive ourselves for all the thoughts and actions that we know are not appropriate to our being. We have to forgive ourselves for not being a more clear reflection of Divine Perfection. We have to forgive others, too, and the very way of things.

Stillness, ultimately, takes surrender. Surrender to that which is beyond our control. Surrender to the stream of life and how it has always streamed without our willing it and how it will continue streaming long after we are gone. The small ego self dissolves in this stream. It is a definite letting go to allow this stream to move through us and change us.

Just as nature goes through periods of gestation and stillness, so we need periods of stillness in our lives. Stillness, while not easy, invites us to examine our lives from the inside out. In stillness, we can stop and take notice of our judgments and inevitable failings and invite a moment of self-love and of loving the depth of experience just as it is.

In stillness, we provide fertile ground for our purpose to unfold.

# Contemplation

Take an inventory of your week and schedule in more time for stillness. Even if the stillness is within, while you are in motion, you can still reap its benefits.

Here are some ideas:

Intentionally focus on the breath while driving or on the train.
Standing in line at the store, focus on all the sounds as one sound.
Take a quiet time to reflect and journal your reflections.
Meditate: sit and focus on the breath for five minutes.
Sit and listen to soothing music.
Take a walk outdoors, focusing on taking unhurried steps.
Practice Tai Chi, a moving meditation.

# Reflections and Wonderings

# 13: Know Your True Nature

World religions and traditions through time have suggested that we are finite as humans as well as infinite and part of a Divine Plan.

In the Christian tradition, as I mentioned earlier, you are known as part of the Body of Christ and as such have unique gifts that you are here to use for the benefit of the greater Body.

In Yoga, your higher nature is the *Atman*, the Ultimate Reality, only your eyes are veiled from this truth. Meditation and prayer help you uncover this awareness of your purest, essential nature.

In many traditions, developed over the thousands of years of human history, we are taught again and again: we are not alone nor are we singular. Our very nature is unified with or even the same as the Infinite.

This seeming contradiction of being small yet infinite can feel confusing to the "small self" that wants its creature comforts *right now* and yet can sense the ultimate futility of being attached to such comforts. We want stability and security *today*. And yet our infinite nature is full of flux and change, continually challenging us to let go of our grasping for security.

Our very nature challenges our sense of self to its roots. We may wonder how we can possibly have a Divine nature when we have so many concerns, tendencies and struggles that seem to veil our knowledge of our very nature.

This is where community is essential to well-being. Religions and traditions throughout the ages also teach that we are here to serve each other. Our nature is not individual, but communal. Service is as varied in nature as people are varied in their interests. But doing what you do from a context of serving your fellow human beings takes the small "me" and puts it into greater context.

The greater "Body" is not an abstract concept, then, but a living, breathing body of people that you interact with and find commonality with and with whom you experience mutual support and understanding.

# Contemplation

Ask yourself, *Who constitutes my community?* This may be family, neighborhood or other communities of choice.

List the ways you already serve these communities.

What aspect of what you do are you drawn to the most? Make links between that aspect and how you are living out your purpose right now.

Journal about any thoughts or promptings you have about serving one or more of these communities in a new and different way.

If you feel overcommitted in the area of serving others, think of something you can let go of and commit to doing one self-loving activity today.

# Reflections and Wonderings

# 14: Express Your Essence

While each of us is fundamentally Divine Essence expressed in a finite body, our expression of this essence is unique. Just as no one has your exact combination of skin, eye color, hair or smile, no one has your exact expression of essence, what we will call your essential nature.

And while this is related to our gifts, it is more related to our essential nature. What makes us tick? As a mom, it has been very interesting observing the children my son plays with. When they were very young, these boys' unique natures shone through loud and clear. One preschool boy enjoyed the sheer physical pleasure of slamming toys against each other and against the floor. An elementary school boy took apart an old computer to find out how it was put together. Another boy loved to imagine things, and he and my son spent afternoons creating complex structures in the sandbox.

These boys' interests as teens have followed their natures. The very kinetic child is taken by the world of soccer and excels at it. The computer explorer competes in robotics competitions. My son and his sandbox buddy are adept in the arts and sciences.

From a very early age, our unique approach to life is revealed. It is who we are at a fundamental level. Remembering what your favorite activities were, or what you did for long stretches of time without wanting to stop, will give you a window into your basic nature.

When I rewind my own tapes I find myself playing in the woods with my friends and sister. I find myself singing and writing. I still love to do these things, and my purpose has unfolded from these very activities. While I have a hard time putting a name to this essential nature, I can feel the tone of it. If I look at photos of myself at a young age, I see this nature quite clearly.

Our nature may shine through more clearly as children. If that does not seem true for you, sometimes the era of coming of age as young teens or adults can also reveal these qualities. As you were coming of age, how did you express yourself through your studies or work or play?

In the unfolding of purpose, this essential nature is what we must return to for purpose to unfold properly. If our essence is somehow packed away and put in a closet, our search for purpose will be very difficult, if not impossible. We must be who we are fundamentally to fully understand what we are here on the planet to do.

# Contemplation

Explore your memories of early childhood, perhaps between four and seven years of age. What occupied your time? See if you can peel back what motivated you in those activities. Was it curiosity about the physical world? Did you like to help other people? Did you wonder about the "why" of the world? Were you captivated by a world of imagination?

Find a picture of yourself at this age, or a little older if you cannot find a younger picture. Look into the picture and see if you can remember how it felt to be this age. See if you can feel your essence shining through.

Next, feel who you are now. Is there a difference? If so, sit with the picture every day, drawing your younger self toward you, until you can reclaim that most fundamental essence.

# Reflections and Wonderings

# 15: Placing Your Attention

Simple shifts in where we place our attention can radically alter how we experience our world. Attention can alter the very context of our lives.

The other day, my husband Jonathan and I were driving through Mercer County Park, a 2500-acre park where deer often graze in late afternoon. We were able to stop within about ten feet of two deer who didn't seem to mind our presence, even our voices, as we exclaimed at how friendly they seemed.

I was brought back to when we first moved to our suburban region from New York City. I remember seeing all the dead deer along the side of the road, and being so saddened that my experience of being around greater nature was that I saw its devastation.

Over time, I began to look a little more closely and to see deer standing in corn fields in late afternoon or at the park where I walked. Now, I see them everywhere. At night, I drive slowly down the road that we live on, hoping to catch sight of a doe or a buck in a grove of trees where they are often grazing. Once a symbol of devastation to me, deer have now become companions, symbols of stillness and natural beauty.

How we feel about our surroundings or the people we love and interact with has a lot to do with where we are placing our attention. We can choose to focus on our circumstances with a higher intent to understand or we can lock in on its flaws. It's a choice that shapes our very experience of these circumstances.

Where we place our attention begins with habits that we form as children or patterns we get into over the years, but it is truly a choice. In the unfolding of purpose, notice often where you are placing your attention.

Are you placing the majority of your day's attention on destructive or constricted elements of your life circumstances and surroundings, or are you seeking out what is alive and flourishing?

# Contemplation

Take stock of your work, health, relationships and mental habits. What is working and what is not working?

In the areas that are not working, write down one simple change in perception that would help this area to work better. For example, if you hate your job, ask yourself: what am I learning through this experience? Are you being asked to be more vocal about your needs or more receptive to the needs of others? Usually we are exactly where we are because we are being offered a chance to grow.

If you are in a tough relationship, try to see the highest intent of the other person. Is that intent to connect to you? Is that intent to experience love? Sometimes the toughest shift in perspective is shifting toward self-love and setting a self-loving boundary in a relationship.

Do you see yourself as healthy or unhealthy? If you see yourself as unhealthy, focus on all of the ways that your body works miraculously to keep you on this plane. Offer gratitude to your body for the ways it works.

Are there times that you spiral into negative thinking? Are there certain times of days or certain people that trigger this thinking? See if you can use the breath to interrupt this thinking when it happens and bring you back to the present moment. Try substituting a mantra or positive statements to replace these habits.

Here are a few cleansing mantras that I have employed to interrupt negative mental habits:

"The Lord is my shepherd, I have everything I need" — the 23rd Psalm of the Bible
"Lord, make me an instrument of thy peace" — St. Francis
"Om Mani Padme Hung" — a Tibetan Buddhist prayer of compassion

# Reflections and Wonderings

# 16: Perception and Reality

It is true that what we focus on significantly changes what we see and how we see the world around us. It changes what shows up in our world. On the path of understanding our purpose, it is important to take stock of how we *perceive* where we are and what we are doing in our lives.

Seen one way, everything in our lives emerges as prompts to follow purpose more fully or nudges us to awaken to the Divine nature within us more completely. Seen this way, there is never anything wrong or incomplete about where we are right now and what we are experiencing. Everything is just as it should be, and we learn as we go along how to shift and change according to what is arising.

That said, it is difficult to hold this view for sustained periods of time. This is where practice is useful. When we practice shifting our perception toward accepting what is and seeing life as a learning process, the practice itself changes our perception and the habits of our mind.

As we make these shifts in perception, what we are willing to invite into our lives also shifts. We may find that as our perception shifts, life shifts with it.

The great adage, "what you focus on grows," is taught in the human potential movement as a means to manifest what your heart desires in the future. The confusion that this often brings is that when "bad" things happen, we wonder if we somehow brought this on ourselves.

This is a common misunderstanding of this principle. While we do affect our reality through our choices and attitudes, we are part of an immense web of dynamic creation and evolution that began at the beginning of the world, and probably before that. While we are responsible for our decisions, there are tens of thousands of factors that determine what shows up in our lives on any given day. So what does it mean that shifting perception can shift what shows up for us?

An obvious example is to see loved ones or colleagues in a new light. Focusing on the higher self of that person rather than annoying flaws will alter how you relate to this person. And as you relate differently, what shows up between you becomes a completely different dynamic. Something may grow from that which you never expected.

On the path of understanding purpose, if you focus every day on finding and creating meaning, in the smallest choices you make, this will help open doorways for more significant movement.

## Contemplation

Commit to shifting one dynamic in your life right now. It may be with a relationship to a person or a job or a community you are a part of. If you have habitual negative thinking concerning this area, commit to raising the bar of your awareness. Consider the person or circumstance for what you are learning from it, and put that learning into action.

If it is speaking out more clearly about your needs or truth, then begin to speak out more clearly. If it is creating a self-loving boundary and commanding more respect, then create that self-loving boundary. If it is organizing and sprucing up your office so that you have a better feeling about where you work, then do that. This is about shifting dynamics. Consider journaling your observations about how this new dynamic shifts both your inner perspective and your external experience in this area.

# Reflections and Wonderings

# Part Two

# Doorways

# to Purpose

# 17: Be Where You Are

In talking about purpose, I am drawn to the image of the flower that blooms from the bud. It is a slow, delicate unfolding that cannot be rushed. That said, sometimes we get hung up on what our process looks like, and we may feel that we are not "getting anywhere." I spoke earlier of honoring the process. Where you are now is where you are meant to be on your path. Everything that you are experiencing now is shaping who you will be tomorrow.

So even though you may feel lost, you are not lost. When you feel lost, you are in the process of being found. Often, we must be encounter this uncomfortable feeling of unknowing in order to have the openness of heart for something new to unfold. Our unfolding is naturally intelligent.

Those who are living out their purpose will tell you that they, too, felt lost at one time. And they still may have moments of feeling lost or steeped in unknowing. But these experiences all move us toward embracing our purpose more fully, with ever stronger and wider arms.

Just at the bud of a flower is a gathering of energy that is just about to expand, you are right now gathering energy for your next expansion.

The next step of your purpose is most often a deep integration of everything you have learned up to this point in your life. So there is no judging where you are now. You are in a period of integration and gathering energy. That is exactly as it should be.

The search to understand our purpose is fundamentally a search to understand our essential nature, which is always present and yet always evolving. The deepest meaning in life is found in uncovering this essential nature. This is why the Indian saint Ramana Maharshi taught, "Be as you are." We can add to that: "Be where you are."

# Contemplation

Write out how you feel right now about your purpose in life. Do you feel lost in a dark wood? Do you wonder if you ever will find your way? Maybe you know your purpose but are wondering how to bring it about in the world.

Journal these question:
If I am supposed to be somewhere else now, where would that be?
What would my life look like?

You may have a vivid image in your mind of what that looks like. Pay attention to that. That is useful information in the path of unfolding purpose.

Now imagine you are there, in that place of being. Are you a different person than you are now? How different, and different in what ways?

The point of this exercise is to get out that inner voice of "should" so that you can be free from it.

Close your eyes and imagine you are in a dark wood and lost. A voice pervades the darkness that is loving and gentle and deeply accepting of you just the way you are, right now in this moment.

The voice says, "Be just as you are. Be right where you are."

Sit and allow this voice and sentiment to bathe your being. Breathe.

# Reflections and Wonderings

# 18: What Do You Long For?

When we go down deep enough into the longing of the heart, we find the seed of life itself. In this place, we are no longer singular but are one seed in the great flower of life. This is the place where we disappear and a larger Presence moves through us. For the sake of speaking about purpose, we can think of this point of union as the *seed of life* from which purpose sprouts.

This seed of life contains your life purpose and is bursting at the seams. Correct conditions will nurture its growth. When you are trapped in mental thinking, the ground for this seed's growth becomes dry and harsh. The seed of your life and purpose grows in difficult and strenuous conditions.

When you drop the mental noise, through heart listening and mindfulness practice, there is a fountain that begins to flow. This fountain of the heart waters the seed of your life and purpose. You begin to prosper.

The mind will want to control your life and the seed of your purpose. The mind does not like to let go of control. But for purpose to unfold correctly, the mind must surrender and become the servant of the heart.

One of the traps in the path toward understanding purpose is a belief that the purpose will unfold through thinking about it. While there are exercises to contemplate purpose in this book, these are exercises to help you refine what you are listening for. Purpose ultimately unfolds through our heart's longing, not through mental thinking. So spend time deepening your awareness of what your heart is longing for.

A way of discovering this is to sit with your attention on your heart, in a quiet place. Do you sense a longing or a deep desire for something you can't quite name? This may be a longing for your destiny. Or put another way, it may be a longing to experience that union of the finite and infinite that our purpose draws us toward.

There are ten thousand doors that lead to your purpose manifested in the world. One of these doors is to listen to this longing. Your longing is the desire of this seed within to burst and become expressed fully in your life. It is a deep calling of the soul for expression.

## Contemplation

What do you long for? Write down all of the things that you long for. These may at first come out as a job, a more passionate relationship, money, freedom. Then go underneath these surface manifestations and ask yourself why you want these things. See if you can get to a more essential longing. This may have to do with creative expression, freedom to express your thoughts or ideals, freedom to lead; whatever it is write it down and pay attention to this longing as you move forward through your exploration.

# Reflections and Wonderings

# 19: What Do You Love?

The great naturalist John Muir said that when he went out for a walk, he would stay out until sundown, because "going out was really going in." He saw his relationship with nature as a relationship with all things, including his own inner being. He is said to have loved nature like a devotee. Because of Muir's love and devotion to nature, national natural treasures are preserved in Yosemite Valley and Sequoia National Park and other areas.

It is common for us to question doing what we love. Perhaps we have been told that what we love is not practical. Perhaps we look around and see how much work would be required to make a living at doing something non-traditional. But the truth is that the desire to do what we love is the very prompting of our souls to bring what we love about in the world. It is a prompting to increase the presence of love and care in the world.

I'm just going to repeat that because it is something that is so often missed in how we conduct our lives. *Doing what we love increases the very presence of love in the world.* The yoga chant master Krishna Das says that he began offering chant as a way to remember what it felt like to sit at the feet of his guru, whom he studied with in India. His driving desire was to abide in that presence of love he experienced with his guru. Now, he travels the world, nurturing this quality of abiding love in others through his music.

When we follow that inner prompting, we go out in the world and into our truest self at the same time. We become timeless beings, following a path that has been prepared for us before we were even aware of it. As I have mentioned elsewhere, as we focus on what is important to us, the world around us shifts. It is as if Infinite Intelligence showers us with *YES*!

As John Muir found, doing what we love is a portal through which we find a quality of spaciousness that holds all of life. It may be love of trees, or love of your culture. It may be love of people gathered for a cause, or love of music. When we fully devote ourselves to what or whom we love, this space opens in our hearts. In this kind of immersion, the mind drops its worry about the future, and can let go into a deeper quality of space and time.

It is not selfish or impractical or difficult to do what you love. It is your soul's imperative!

# Contemplation

What do you love? Take one hour to completely immerse yourself in an activity you love but haven't done for a while.

Take note of how you feel beforehand, and then take note of how you feel afterward.

If you are unsure of what activity this might be, look back into your childhood. What did you do that made you feel alive? Do that activity, even if it is swinging or playing in the sandbox!

# Reflections and Wonderings

# 20: What Is Your Delight?

Another way of investigating what you love is asking yourself what brings you delight. Delight is similar to love except that it may feel even a little more indulgent! When we think of what we love, we may also feel a sense of duty. Delight, however, is a quality of heart that is very light and child-like. When we delight in something, our heart opens in celebration, and we become part of this experience in a way that borders on bliss.

When a child delights in a ball, the child is moved by the bounding energy of only that single ball. The child thinks of nothing but experiencing how the ball bounces, how it moves. When we delight in our work, or in our relationships, or in our creative pursuits, we are absorbed in these activities in a similar way. Our hearts are open; we are present and joyful.

Especially during times when we experience difficulty, it is important to do what delights us. When we spend time doing activities that bring us delight, we become more buoyant, and that buoyancy rubs off on those around us. Tapping our delight gives us energy and creativity.

In the process of trying to understand your purpose, spending time in doing what delights you keeps your heart open for the journey.

In helping people with purpose exploration, a perspective I have encountered is that to do what we delight in feels selfish. I want to establish here that following a trail of delight can open your world to purpose simply *because* it is of the self. It is self-*ish*. Because delight is of the deepest Self that longs for expression, it can bring pure magic. People are following a singular delight all of the time and making huge impacts in their world.

Here I think of young Olympic athletes who inspire not only those in their immediate circle, but the world over. I think of Bono and his band U2, whose music inspires generations of listeners and whose compassionate advocacy has continued untold impact. I think of Oprah whose influence would take pages to describe. Then there are those in your immediate circle who are following paths that draw on an innate sense of delight in what they do. Consider their impact on you and others in your community.

When we delight in something, it is contagious. As a child delights in a ball, a parent or other onlooker delights in the child's experience. I think of the words of Christ, that you must be like little children to enter the Kingdom of Heaven. A child's world is full of delight. When we delight in something or someone, our hearts are open, and we experience a little piece of heaven in that moment.

The most important thing to remember is that when you enter this heaven even for a moment, you bring back a little of it to share with others. What may seem selfish from the outside is the most selfless thing you could do.

Do what delights you. Let your purpose begin with delight.

## Contemplation

Delight is found in the heart, in the cherished moment of walking toward life with arms wide open. Here are some questions to consider as you go through your day or as you journal:

How do you open your arms to life? What is your delight?

Is it taking photographs? Is it talking with a child? Is it golfing? Is it making something with your hands? Is it talking on the phone with a friend?

If you do not know, go back in time to when you were a child or a young adult, and see if you can find a burst of joy there. What was it that made your heart open?

Commit to spending one hour per day or week in this activity. If you feel you have no time, consider how life is without spending time doing what delights you. See if you can make it a priority, so that you can reap the many rewards of a moment spent in the space of delight.

# Reflections and Wonderings

# 21: Delight and Purpose

Delight can show us our purpose, as it may be the very thing that brings us in union with our deeper self, the place of Divine Purpose. We've talked about the timelessness that comes when you do what you love or delight in. "I lose myself" is a thing that people often say when they are involved in something they find delight in. "I lose track of time."

When you lose yourself and lose track of time, you are present to the moment. You are dwelling in the realm of deep delight, which is the realm of the Spirit. You may dwell so deeply here that delight may not even arise as an emotion, but a place of inward dwelling and peace.

When you lose yourself, you also find yourself in a new way. When you lose yourself – you lose this small entity called "self" or "I" – you merge with something much greater and eternal. This is Essence, God, Life, *Atman*, The space of *I Am*.

The question of "what is my purpose?" then becomes a question of what you delight in that takes you to this place of forgetting yourself and losing yourself to something greater. In what setting do you lose yourself (or are you willing to lose yourself) so that you become aware of the greater Self that moves through you?

Explore what brings you delight. It may not be just one thing. It may be a host of things. Purpose can be described as an unfolding of what is "ours to do" here on the planet. The truth is, we have many, many things to do. Many things may bring us delight and joy and a sense of meaning and purpose. In this exploration, watch for what brings you the *most* delight.

When we do these things that delight us, we enter a place of inner peace, even if it is temporary. As that peace changes us, it emanates to those around us, and we are changed together. Delight is deeply purposeful.

# Contemplation

Imagine you are an investigative cinematographer, reviewing the footage of your experiences in life so far, from childhood to now. You are looking for activities that have brought you delight and a sense of timelessness and that have *persisted throughout your life*. Some examples:

Traveling
Day-dreaming
Night dreaming
Golfing
Knitting
Singing
Woodworking
Shopping
Skiing
Playing Football
Roller Skating

You get the idea. There are limitless possibilities. If you still have access to this activity, spend some time this week immersing yourself in it. Even if you feel you will never have enough time to do this activity as much as you like, do it anyway. You are feeding your soul when you do an activity like this. You are tending the soil in which your purpose can grow.

Keep these questions about delight at the forefront as you move through the various exercises in this book.

# Reflections and Wonderings

# 22: Do What You Love

Steering yourself toward what you love will most likely mean giving up things that you hold less dear. There is a knot that often needs to be untied when you are ready to do what you love. This knot is the combination of *resistance* to doing what you love paired with all the things that you *fill your time with* that are *not* doing what you love. Having a clear, stated intention to do what you love can help ease this knot and begin its undoing.

Before I was clear about the purpose of my writing, I found thousands of things to fill my time that had nothing to do with what I loved doing—writing. I know how hard it is to turn toward what you love. It takes risking failure, even risking success! It takes all of your inner gusto to turn toward what you love. It may mean risking income, risking a relationship or even risking your sense of who you are—your self-identity.

Undoing the knot of resistance and time-filling is not easy. But with intention and awareness, it is possible. The first step is to give yourself permission to do what you love and delight in. Often people come to me with an idea of what they want to do and are simply looking for confirmation or permission. This is not surprising, as it is difficult to see oneself clearly without reflection from our external world. But if you know what you want to do, and it is only about permission, then I am here to say: you have permission! In fact I will shout it from the mountaintops: YOU HAVE PERMISSION!

One of the greatest things about purpose is that when you become aligned with a higher purpose, time has a way of expanding. This doesn't mean that you are not busy. But when you do what you love, there is that timeless quality to the doing that I spoke of earlier. So instead of feeling the time crunch in that moment, you actually feel the spaciousness of time. You experience time flowing through your human experience, and you flowing through time. This sense of flow positively affects other areas of your life.

We will talk later about resistance. For now, give yourself permission to follow your heart's deepest love. Give yourself time to do what you love.

# Contemplation

Create a "Love" list. Write down three things you love to do the most (even if you feel they are not related to your purpose).

Now below this, write a "Giving up" list. List three things that waste time and that you are willing to give up so that you can pursue what you love. Post this somewhere so you can see it every day.

Now in your journal, write down all of the reasons you have internalized for not doing what you love (*It's too late, I'm too old, there's not enough money in it,* that sort of thing).

Write down your intention to follow your truest love, even if you do not yet know what it is.

If you feel inspired, create a large sign for yourself and post it somewhere, reminding you to do what you know you love the most!

# Reflections and Wonderings

# 23: Letting Old Wood Burn

As uncomfortable as it is, loss of the familiar is an invitation to transform from the inside out. It is an invitation to rekindle our lives.

I have been building fires for years, either in my fireplace in winter or while camping in summer. Fires invite introspection, or at least quietude, and there are times in our lives when we are more drawn toward this quietude than other times. Often external difficulty, whether in the form of a loss of income, a necessary move or a loss of a loved one, prompts us to draw our energy inward and regroup.

When you burn wood, you rely on the coals of that wood to ignite the new logs that you put on the fire. If the old wood does not burn down, there are no coals to keep the fire going. Similarly, when the old parts of our lives are burned down through loss or change, whether we choose it or not, we have the coals needed to keep the fire of life going. Simultaneously, we have an opportunity to put new "logs" on the fire.

The mind has the tendency to want to cling to the old and familiar. But trust is a quality that can reside deeper than the mind's worries; it is a gut-level clinging to faith despite the fury of the mind's doubts. If we can trust the letting go, we can open ourselves to transformation and a reigniting of life.

This can happen on a personal level, and it can happen on a collective level. As a country and globe, as we collectively regroup from losses of jobs and financial security, from changing and uncertain habitat, and continued loss of life through war and poverty, we have the opportunity to make new choices. There is intelligence in the transformation taking place right now. The "burning down" of the old is never easy. It asks us to understand that life is in a continual process of transformation, and it asks us to participate consciously in the process.

The mythical phoenix rises from the ashes of its own destruction, flapping its beautiful wings of hope. Right now, we are the phoenix, as individuals and as a country and as a planet. What new bird will rise? What wings are growing that will soar into the future?

# Contemplation

If you have experienced a major loss, take time to contemplate what new wings have grown out of it. If it is a loss of a job or feeling of security, contemplate what new opportunities are before you. If it is loss of health or the health of a loved one, ask yourself if there are wings of hope arising for a new diet or lifestyle or way of relating. If it is loss of a loved one, whether through death, a move or a break-up, take some time to look within to see if there are wings of that person's spirit in your heart.

On the other hand, perhaps nothing is changing and you feel stuck or stagnant. If that is the case, look around your life and living space and see if there is something you can consciously change. Perhaps you can get rid of some old furniture in storage. Perhaps you can speak up in a relationship that needs a new dynamic. Or perhaps you need to create time in your schedule to start a creative project. Change is sometimes difficult, but it does keep the fire of our lives burning bright!

Journal questions:
What makes up the ashes of my life?
What have I lost?
And what are the makings of the phoenix? What is wanting to be born in my life and brought into expression?

# Reflections and Wonderings

# 24: Active Transformation

There is no way to be on a path of understanding your deeper nature and purpose without having to surrender what is no longer appropriate to your being. In some religious traditions, this surrender of the self is established as a practice through the taking of vows to give up sexual partnership, alcohol, material wealth, certain foods or other attachments.

It is guaranteed that as you grow, you will be challenged to let go of not only old belief systems, but old habits and ways of being and relating to work, love, money, community or other aspects of life that arise out of those belief systems and habits. You will be confronted with new circumstances that ask you to either choose to hold onto the belief system and re-create old wounds, or let go of these systems and wounds and act according to what you know to be true.

One method I've found to be useful in letting go is to literally get rid of old things. As I go through my closets and attic and basement, I ask for the "old stuff" of my life to go, too. I become aware of the new that I am providing a space for simply by getting rid of old things.

As a poignant example of this, soon after I wrote these words, I was catching myself at an old habit of working hard and neglecting to nourish my body and soul properly. I began to contemplate what "proper nourishment" would look like for me. That week, I went to the gym and also scheduled in more time for meditation. Yet I knew I could do more. As a cosmic and comic (though not comic at the time) reminder about "proper nourishment" I got a very large and inconvenient reminder—my refrigerator died that week!

Letting go of old habits can actually feel painful, as we step out of our comfort zone and into a new habit, new way of being, new way of responding to the world. But consider the alternative: not letting go of old ways of reacting or responding to our circumstances can create unnecessary suffering. Better to actively create those changes when we are being prompted to do so.

# Contemplation

List one habit of the mind or body that you want to change that you know is getting in the way of helping you understand and carry out your purpose. Write down one new habit that supports your purpose that you want to develop.

Next, find at least three old things in your house and give them away (or throw them out). As you give them away, tell yourself that you are also releasing any old patterns related to this habit to the Divine.

Our local Vietnam Veterans group collects items from our front doorstep as a benefit to their group. Find the community collection program in your area, and begin to let go of old things and old ways! Say a blessing over your stuff, to be sure that the new owners are able to benefit from these items.

Post this new habit somewhere where you can see it, to remind yourself of this change.

Some suggestions:

Letting go of the habit of negative self-talk
Replacing it with the habit of gratitude for aspects of the day
Letting go of filling every minute of the day with activity
Replacing it with the habit of quiet listening
Letting go of the habit of doubting that purpose will be clarified
Replacing it with spending time using positive mantras or prayer

# Reflections and Wonderings

# 25: The Inner Judge

When we were young professionals just starting out in the world, I had long conversations with my sister, Juanita, a professional artist. Together, we would sort through all of the voices that told us that we should be doing more practical things, more community-oriented things, more service-oriented things than writing stories and creating art.

One practice Juanita shared with me at the time was of imagining an overbearing "bishop" on her shoulder when encountering inner judgment. "Thanks for sharing," she'd tell the bishop, then banish him from his post with a flick of her fingers. We grew up in a religious household, so the "bishop" represented the voice of the community who established the rules and oversaw that these rules were followed. Creating an overbearing bishop was her way of dealing with the inner guilt-monger that would have her sacrifice what she truly felt led to do.

We all have voices that we must deal with as we sort out our purpose and how best to follow it. These voices may be internalized voices from our parents, our culture, our religion or our friends. You may know consciously that these voices are completely irrational, and yet still they may have a firm grip on who you allow yourself to be.

Bringing understanding to and then flicking away a negative, self-defeating voice is a helpful way to bring clarity to the voice that you want to prevail—the voice of the heart. The self-defeating voice is often the voice of reason and judgment, squashing the wild, passionate expressions that threaten a sense of safety and security.

Reason and judgment have their uses later as you navigate the choices in bringing your purpose into the world. But on the path toward purpose, the voice of the heart must reign supreme.

# Contemplation

List all of the judgments that you carry about finding and living out your purpose. Those judgments might have to do with lack around money or time, what people will think, what you *should* be doing, etc. Give this judge a personality. If you could embody this judge, what would he or she look like? Imagine a conversation with this judge. Ask this judge what he or she wants.

This exercise helps uncover our shadow self that keeps us from following our purpose. Often the judge wants us to be secure and safe. Having a loving conversation with this part of ourselves can bring inner reassurance that we are okay, no matter what outlandish purpose we may discover.

If you find this judge returning, even after honoring what it had to say, flick that judge away, saying "Thank you for sharing!"

# Reflections and Wonderings

# 26: Mirrors of Your Purpose

Purpose unfolds in our lives like petals of a flower opening one by one. When the people in our lives mirror back what they see unfolding in us, it helps us better understand our purpose and direction.

Ideally, as children, we can clearly know what is unfolding within us because our parents witness what they see and provide us with feedback. They may provide us with this kind of input, "You really seem to enjoy athletics!" Or, "You seem to have a knack for the piano!" Or, "You are naturally compassionate and kind."

As children, our natural gifts may have been encouraged and supported in this way, or they may have been ignored or torn down or overshadowed by a parent's gifts. It is very common for a parent to focus a child's attention on a life path that the parent deems practical or honorable or interesting rather than listening to what is emerging through the child.

As children or young adults, we may have accepted such external feedback or lack of feedback as truth. Without this proper mirroring, we can become confused as to our purpose. If we felt for sure that being a ballerina was our calling, and we were directed toward mathematics, it can create an inner conflict with our own sense of self and what we know to be true about ourselves and our interests.

As adults, we can find more accurate mirrors in friends or family members who are willing to be honest, or we may seek out a skilled mentor. You can ask someone whose honest feedback you respect: What do you see are my gifts? What do you think I would be good at doing? Do you have a hunch about where I am headed? Often those who are closest to us see us more clearly than we see ourselves.

In asking for this kind of feedback, it's important to only take what resonates with you and discard the rest. Adults can also be misdirected by erroneous information!

The key thing to ask yourself in getting feedback is: *what am I hearing that feels like a reflection of what is unfolding in my life and my heart? What feels like a reflection of my highest purpose?* If what you are hearing feels like a "close second" to what you know to be true, then toss this information away. Sometimes even inaccurate information can be helpful, as we may have an inner reaction to it that reveals what we really think.

## Contemplation

Identify one or two people in your life to ask the questions posed above. You may want to come up with additional questions to ask. If there is someone who knew you as a child, start with asking what natural tendencies you showed at a young age that you may not be aware of. Friends or colleagues can also give you feedback as to what they see as your strengths. The information you gather can provide invaluable information for your process.

# Reflections and Wonderings

# 27: A Natural Direction

Like the DNA blueprint of a flower, we each have our "purpose" blueprint. This is made up of our natural tendencies, as well as gifts handed down through the generations. While there may be no "handwriting on the wall" that dictates our purpose, we do have certain trajectories that we can tease out if we look close enough.

Some contemplation of your family lineage and the gifts handed down can be useful in understanding what "material" you are working with in your life. Talk to aunts and uncles, cousins, a brother or sister. What would they say are the family gifts?

We talked about interviewing family and friends about their hunches about you and what they see as your gifts. Now we are looking at family gifts and tendencies. There may be a tendency toward helping others or providing leadership or rallying people or organizing or exploring. Family gifts can be useful in understanding our purpose because we can see ourselves mirrored by the activities of others like us.

Of course, you may feel that you are opposite from your family in every way. But close investigation of your interests and theirs may find some overlap. It is at least worth taking time to inquire. Remember, we often know something by its opposite!

When I was in my twenties, and in a state of confusion about my life's direction, I lived near my grandparents for a year. In that year, which became the subject of my first book, I learned through observation that my father's family has a keen interest in making things and fiddling with the world of objects. This helped put my writing into context. I no longer felt like an odd ball!

Family gifts will be as many and as varied as you have members of your family, so it's important to look at each individual and what they have expressed in their lives.

You may also find people who have avoided their gifts, and if this is the case, consider why they may have made this sacrifice. What was the outcome of this sacrifice? Some contemplation of "why" will help you have compassion for your own journey.

# Contemplation

Take some time to conduct interviews of family, friends and colleagues. Once you complete your interviews, do some reflection on what you see as your gifts, tendencies and family inheritance. What was said that resonates with you?

Then start putting the picture together. Match gifts and family gifts, and other tendencies that were identified, and see what you come up with. It may seem preposterous at first. It doesn't matter if it seems outlandish. You don't have to quit your job and go out and do this tomorrow! This is just useful information on the path toward purpose.

# Reflections and Wonderings

# 28: The Uses of Fear

What you fear is often what you are moving toward. I don't mean fear of death or fear of dogs! I mean fear of something that you are facing, right now, in relationship to your everyday life.

Fear is a form of resistance. It slows down the process of our unfolding purpose so that we can gain strength and clarity through each step of the journey.

Fear is very revealing of direction, like a weathervane. It helps us see which way the wind is blowing. If you look at what you are facing right now and what you fear the most, it is most likely pointing the way for you. If you fear losing or quitting your job, you may be up for a job change. If you fear running out of money and living on the street, you may be up for a new relationship with money and what makes you feel secure. If you fear public speaking, you may want to explore courses in speaking!

On the path toward purpose, fear can be a great teacher.

Facing your fear is an excellent way to explore purpose. I have a client who fears authority and so has embraced studying with a Zen master. In walking straight toward this fear, she is giving herself the chance not only to learn the way of Zen but to undo all of the inner beliefs that support this fear of authority.

We generally think of fear as a negative emotion. If we are controlled by it, yes, it can have a negative impact. But when seen as a teacher, it can lead us toward a greater understanding of our purpose. In my own path, moving toward what I fear the most, I have experienced how fear can feel like a gate buzzing with a thousand hornets. There is just no way you want to go through that. Yet once through the gate and safely on the other side, you see how those hornets are only figments of your imagination, mere shadows.

Fear is only a teacher, a passageway, an invitation.

# Contemplation

What do you fear most? List all of your major fears, especially as they relate to your purpose. Then write down the reasons you have these fears. Pick one of these fears, one that feels like you are ready to walk toward it. Commit to facing this fear through a real-world action.

Is it public speaking? Join Toastmasters!

Is it singing in public? Go to church and during a hymn, sit in a front pew and sing your part loudly.

Is it fear of quitting a job? Imagine this day in your mind. Why are you quitting? What do you fantasize doing? Pay attention to that answer—it's all information to lead you toward purpose.

If it is death, then take some time to imagine your funeral. Imagine your body, your remains. This may seem morose, but it is a time-honored practice. Imagine what is said about you. This can give you helpful information in finding out what is most important to you. What will be said about you that is passed down through the generations? How does that relate to your purpose?

# Reflections and Wonderings

# 29: The Uses of Envy

Envy is also a great teacher. If we envy something, we desire it so greatly that it creates the twisted, gnarled gripping feeling within us that we call envy. It's an unpleasant feeling, and one that we are usually ashamed of. But envy is an ally on the path toward purpose.

Just think for a moment about the people you envy. I don't mean the people whose stuff you envy; I mean the people you envy. If you take a good look at the people you envy, you will find a relationship between those people and where you are headed with your purpose.

For example, when I started contemplating this question, I realized I envied certain authors or leaders in the human potential movement. When coming across an article about these individuals, there would be this physical pang. That's useful information!

In envying others, we see our potential played out on an external stage. Envy is our signal that this is a stage that we want to be on, too.

If your envy is spread far and wide, then look at who you envy the *most*. Look for the greatest degree of envy, and you will probably find a commonality between what that person does and your potential. If not, then you may simply be envying the capacity. If this is the case, then you may be looking at your own level of capacity, should you choose to open yourself to being used to that degree.

It is also useful to contemplate who you are not envious of. This shows you areas you may as well not bother contemplating for your purpose in the world. If you are considering a certain line of work, ask yourself if you envy the people who do this kind of work every day. If you don't have even the faintest feeling of wanting to be in those shoes, then you might rethink this choice. Sometimes we might like the *idea* of doing something or like what doing that activity might give us in terms of status, wealth or credibility rather than wanting to actually do this activity every day.

Envy, of course, is not a place to dwell. When you acknowledge the usefulness of envy, this acknowledgement actually helps to let it go. It has served its purpose! You can thank your envy for its usefulness. It has left you green with possibility!

# Contemplation

Who are you envious of the most? List three top people you envy the most for their impact in the world. Remember, this is not about stuff; this is about contribution. These are not people you admire for their immense accomplishments like Mother Teresa or Ghandi. These are people who you envy. When you think of them, you feel that twisted knot of a feeling that is downright uncomfortable.

Write down who you envy. Be specific: name names!

List all of the reasons that you envy them. What qualities in them do you envy and what contributions have they made that make you envious?

Be honest!

List all of the similar ways that you want to contribute to the world.

Detail your similar qualities or desire for similar qualities.

This will give you useful information about your purpose or capacity!

# Reflections and Wonderings

# 30: Imagine

Visualization can be a unique tool for understanding your purpose and imagining how it may be played out in the world.

When I sit with people looking for their next step in the unfolding of their purpose, I often lead them in a visualization exercise to find the answers within. The most common response that I get after doing these exercises is, "I think I'm making this up!"

And it's true: what we see is made up. But it is made up on the most fundamental level, so that if you question it, you question the very foundation of your being. What is this level?

Imagination is like a window into that place where we are all connected. Some call it the unified field of awareness. I like to use the word Presence. When I do visualizations with people, it is uncanny how often what I am guided to say resonates with an image or an idea or even something physical in that person's life at that moment.

Imagination is like a pair of wings, taking us into a place far more expansive than the rational mind. Imagination, when applied for the use of seeking deeper wisdom, takes us into unification with the mind of God.

Visualization gives light and substance to those inner parts of ourselves that we can't easily grasp. *Why do I have so much fear around finding my purpose? How can I know if pursuing my passion is right for me?* I have worked with people on these questions using visualization because it helps us get a handle on what's going on in that mysterious place we call the soul!

Of course, in doing visualizations of your life, you need discernment as to how far you want to go in following what you've visualized, and this is where the rational mind can be of great service. If you imagine quitting your job tomorrow but you have bills to pay, this is where your grounded knowledge of your situation helps you discern correct timing.

It is easy to see why you might fear your imagination. No one wants to build a life on an ungrounded fantasy. But when you do visualization with a higher purpose in mind, your imagination is a tool for a deeper connection, a deeper Imagining.

# Contemplation

Try this visualization to help uncover your purpose. You may want to keep this book handy to write down any impressions that you may receive.

Sit comfortably with your spine straight and take some deep breaths to relax your body and mind. Imagine a set of stairs that leads from your heart down into your belly. Ask, as you walk down these set of stairs, for guidance in helping you understand your purpose clearly. When you get to the bottom of the stairs, imagine a door, and open the door so that you can walk through. Walk through this door into a field of light and air. It is sunny, and there are no clouds. A pond appears, and you go and sit next to the pond.

Now, imagine that you can actually see a figure who symbolizes the Divine for you (such as Christ, the Buddha, etc.) Take your time in imagining this Presence before you. Your imagination is an invitation. When you have a sense of this figure being present, ask the questions that are most pressing about your purpose. When you have finished, thank this Divine Being, and walk through the door, close it and back up the stairs. Breathe deeply.

Write down everything you experienced. Even if you only have a few sense impressions that you experienced, write these down. Everything you experience in this kind of exercise is useful in understanding your purpose.

# Reflections and Wonderings

# 31: The Heart's Doorway

What do you know about your purpose? What have you always known but have been afraid to admit? What secret wish do you have tucked away, all the way down at the bottom of your heart?

Your heart may know more than you think it does. Your secrets may be more important than you think they are. These knowings, which can sound like faint inner whispers or recurring ideas, are the promptings of your soul to awaken those aspects of yourself that are ready to blossom.

The heart is exceedingly intelligent. It is irrational and intuitive and the place where our truest and most brilliant contributions are born. Albert Einstein, one of history's greatest thinkers, said that our society has gotten it backwards. "The intuitive mind is a sacred gift," he said, "and the rational mind is a faithful servant. We have created a society that honors the servant and has forgotten the gift."

If you are searching for purpose, now is the time to remember the treasure you were born with but have ignored, neglected or simply forgotten. Now is the time to remember your sacred gift.

The most important findings in the search for purpose are what you already sense to be true about what you need, where you are headed and how you can be used to best serve your community. When you embrace the sacred gift of your own intuitive knowledge, you begin the blessed and guided journey of being an instrument of a deeper Truth.

Because most of us need external mirrors of our purpose to see ourselves clearly, it is of course useful to share these knowings with a respected friend or family member. However, if you meet up against a rational mind that wants to quash your knowing, *beware!*

Life is full of illusion. It is common that we chase the dreams others feel we should be chasing only to find ourselves lost in a forest created by illusion. To find your way out, you must listen to the promptings of the intuitive heart. Then ask friends and mentors to support you on your outward journey.

The doorway to the heart is always open. Walk through this doorway. You will find the All that is standing within, whispering to you the secrets of your truest and most universal self. Listen, and embrace the purpose that is pulsing with your every heartbeat.

# Contemplation

Sit with your hands over the center of your chest, or the heart center. Breathe in and breathe out deeply until your breath becomes slow and at ease. Imagine that you are sitting in the space of this heart center. It is spacious and dark, much like a cave. Imagine that in this cave a bright being appears next to you. It is a representative of Presence, as in the last exercise. Ask this representative to tell you what you need to know about your purpose today. Ask specific questions. When you receive an answer, make note of it for later. When you are finished, bow your head in gratitude (and praise!) for this guidance. Make an offering of thanks and praise on your counter, table or prayer altar such as a bouquet of flowers, a bowl of colorful fruit or a lit candle. Write down a way to integrate this knowledge immediately into your life, and commit to doing it. Action born of this kind of listening is a living offering of gratitude and praise.

Consider sharing this exercise and what you have learned with a trusted friend or mentor for help discerning its meaning and application.

If you find yourself doubting what knowledge you have gathered, consider these additional words from the great scientist: "Imagination is more important than knowledge. For knowledge is limited to all we now know and understand, while imagination embraces the entire world, and all there ever will be to know and understand."

# Reflections and Wonderings

# 32: A Conversation With God

As you seek your purpose in the world, there are many ways to ask the Divine for guidance. The important thing is to be specific in your asking and to listen carefully for an answer.

One of the more direct ways of asking and listening is creating a question and answer period with the Divine. To do this correctly, I suggest a quiet place where you will not be interrupted. All phones and electronic devices are off. A candle, an altar, a picture or some other reminder of the sacredness of your journey signals to your mind to quiet and go inward. A journal or this book can help you create ground for this conversation to unfold. You may want to begin with some deep breaths to relax your mind.

You might begin with a request such as "Please show me the way."

Listen for a response. Often the first response is the one you want to record. If you find a negative voice that says, "This is ridiculous," you may want to have a conversation with this part of your awareness until you can bring your focus back to listening to a deeper prompting.

You may ask directly, "What is my purpose?" You may also ask about particular areas that interest you that you need some clarity on.

I have guided individuals in such conversations, and it is always enlightening. It has led some clients directly to their purpose in one session. Even if you feel you are accessing an inner voice that is other than the voice of Divine Presence, you are still getting information about your purpose that can help your process.

One spiritual practice is to go into a wilderness area or take a time of fasting to listen for this answer. While this takes extra planning and commitment, it can have powerful results. In 2005, I did a vision quest on Mt. Rainier for four days to do such listening. While it was inconvenient to pack my bags and leave my son and husband for four days, it was one of the most clarifying four days of my entire life.

However you choose to have this conversation, I recommend journaling answers, as the mind can be very doubtful of this conversation later. Having a written record of it can help overcome these doubts when they arise.

# Contemplation

Take time to have a conversation with God about your purpose.

Ask any follow-up questions you want to ask about funding, first steps, best directions.

When you get to an answer that has an emotional impact, such as a feeling of intense fear or intense joy or sadness (or all three all at once!), pay attention by underlining that answer. The emotional body is good at giving us clues about our purpose!

At the end of the conversation, you may want to ask for a sign in the real world. Ask for a small but simple confirmation. Then watch for signs such as visitations from insects or birds, notes in the mail, words from friends, etc., that resonate with the results you received in this conversation. Don't be attached to receiving this confirmation. It is only a request.

# Reflections and Wonderings

# 33: Ask and Receive

At this point, you may have a beginning understanding of your purpose and want to start testing it through real-world action. Getting clear on what it is that you want helps clear the pathway to it. Is it support to carry out your purpose? Is it taking steps to landing a different job? Is it further clarity?

One of the greatest spiritual principles guiding us as we evolve as humans, I believe, is *Ask and you shall receive, seek and you shall find.* This principle was taught by Christ to his disciples as encouragement to them to seek the filling of their hearts with the Holy Spirit.

This "filling" of the Spirit into our lives is the very thing we are talking about when we talk about purpose. We want to unify our lives with the flow of the greater Spirit through action. Asking and receiving of the Beloved opens the heart in a way that simple action or intention-setting does not do. When you ask, you surrender yourself to the grace of a greater Giving.

Getting clear on what your heart desires is the first and fundamental step in being able to receive what it is that you are looking for. When you become clear on what you are looking for, you open your heart to receiving it. Often we don't ask for the fulfillment of our heart's deepest desire because we don't know what it is, or we have somehow lost track of it.

By now, if you have been working through the exercises in this book, you may at least have a sense of what it is that you want or are feeling prompted to do. It is important to act on even the tiniest glimmer of knowledge in this area.

*Ask.* Ask and you will receive. Asking sets a clear intention in the heart that is heard on many levels of your being and by unseen help. When you ask, ask in prayer for the highest outcome for yourself and all beings. This is key to true prosperity of heart and to the most aligned material prosperity. If you have no idea what you are asking for, you can ask simply: *Show me the Way.*

All seeking, ultimately, draws us back into the arms of Infinite Love that resides in our hearts and in the hearts of others. When you ask, you find that the Beloved is already speaking a reply. When you knock, you find that the door of the Spirit is already open.

# Contemplation

Be clear on what it is exactly that you want to invite into your life. Then ask for this in your heart. Make it a vivid and clear asking.

Next, ask yourself: how can I pursue this in the world? What are the things I need to do to invite this into my life and make it my reality?

Commit to doing one thing daily or weekly that will begin to cultivate what it is that you want in your life.

Below is a simple prayer to align the personal self with the Infinite Self today and every day.

A Prayer for Proper Intention

Infinite One,
Show me what is real.
Let me let go of the worries
That consume me and instead
Let me be consumed by
Your Divine Love, your Divine Heart.
Do not let me run away from you
In my thoughts or in my deeds.
Instead, let me serve you with
Every thought and every breath.
Show me the way,
O Lover of the Universe,
My truest Self, my truest Heart.

# Part Three

## A Passionate

## Calling

# 34: Heroes and Role Models

Almost all of us have experienced the inspiration that comes when we see others who are following their passion and living out their purpose. And yet when it comes to making changes to understand and follow our own purpose, we may find ourselves at a loss. We may feel that it is too late, or we are too uncertain, or we are afraid of how the changes might impact our livelihood or relationships.

Tapping into what and who inspires us can help us garner energy for the journey as well as illuminate an aspect of what we are here to do.

If you are particularly inspired by leaders in the arts, you may want to look into how you can be involved in this arena. If you tend to be most inspired by leaders in sports, you may want to investigate careers that have to do with physical health or fitness. If you are inspired by leaders in politics, then investigating how you can get involved in the political or cultural arena could be very useful.

It is not always the case that who inspires us will indicate where we are headed in particular. However, if we investigate what it is about these role models who inspire us, we can gather information for our own purpose.

Reading articles or biographies can also give us inspiration as well as real-world guidance. What obstacles did your hero or role model have to overcome? What winding path did others take to follow their purpose? In considering who they are as people and what challenges they have overcome, our eyes and hearts are opened to new possibilities.

Inspiration ultimately opens our hearts to Divine Guidance. It draws us toward the light and energy of Divine Essence that we see expressed through these particular, human vessels. As we are drawn to these figures, we are drawn to that place inside our own being that contains this same Essence. We see and understand ourselves more clearly.

Role models and heroes call on that place in us that knows that when we follow our highest aspirations, we do so for ourselves as well as for our families, communities and our world. We do so even for the generations to come. Drawing on these inspirational figures in our lives, whether living or no longer here in body, we gain essential support for living out a purposeful life.

# Contemplation

Inspire yourself! Write a vivid statement of who you are and what is important and purposeful in your life right now. Use whatever information you have collected so far and go with it. In this exercise, write quickly and imaginatively. Now write down all of the things that you want do in your life before you die. Write down all of the places you want to go, where you want to live. Write down people you want to meet, or things that you want to do. Write down how you want to make a contribution to others in your life and the legacy you would like to leave for the next generation. No judgment! Just write it all out, vividly.

In this exercise, you must let your imagination and inner guidance have its say. There are so many voices we listen to daily that keep us safe and secure, and yet purpose exploration is about waking us up to new realities! Inspiration comes most easily when you stretch the mind and wake up the senses.

# Reflections and Wonderings

_____

_____

_____

_____

_____

_____

_____

_____

_____

_____

_____

_____

# 35: Sensing Your Capacity

Divine Purpose is a dynamic that is created when we, as small bright vessels, open ourselves up to become channels of the much larger Divine Presence. As vessels, we allow ourselves to embody a Beingness whose capacity is much greater than our own singular capacity.

When we consider our purpose we may feel overwhelmed by the responsibility of making a larger contribution than we already are. We may feel a lack of capacity. However, if we consider that we are only small vessels for a bigger capacity, then we can have no worries about capacity! We are only instruments of a more expansive Presence.

We are told by many spiritual traditions that the Presence of the Divine is as close as our breath and resides in our own hearts. Christ called God *Abba,* which is akin to our *Daddy.* In the Quran, Allah is said to be closer to us than our jugular vein. Contemplate how the Divine could be closer to you than this vein! This is not a formal, arms-length relationship. It is intimate, here, now, within.

This Presence is loving and gentle, yet very powerful! This is the Presence that is guiding our purpose, prompting us to unfold so that we can understand and embrace the temple of Spirit that we are.

We sometimes get glimpses of this deeper, filling Presence in times of great transition. At a birth or wedding, this Presence may fill the room with a quality of stillness, love or intimacy. At the death of a loved one, we may feel this Presence in the form of the sudden preciousness of our own life and the lives of those who remain close to us.

But we can also find this Presence in daily life. Through practicing stillness, mindfulness, artistic expression or other activity to which we put our full, undivided attention, a deeper Presence can open up. This Presence is always available—our only task is to open our awareness and ask what is being required of us.

# Contemplation

How do you cultivate the experience of Presence? Write down the last three times that you've experienced Divine Presence, or a deeper quality of existence that feels timeless. We've talked about stillness and mindfulness, but Presence can open up in highly active moments such as running or having dinner with friends or working on your computer. What is it that evokes your feeling of Presence?

Artistic expression, communion with nature, meditation, and prayer to the Divine are common ways that human beings have experienced Presence throughout time and culture. Are you drawn to one of these areas? Choose an activity to cultivate Presence and practice it this week, without any attachment to outcome. Simply open yourself to the experience.

This is about creating movement so that you can begin to sense the innate capacity and support you have to carry out your purpose.

# Reflections and Wonderings

# 36: What You Have Found

As you do this exploration, you are asking and allowing for the truest parts of who you are to be revealed. As you confront fears and face worries, you may find that you are willing to be more (or less!) of a risk-taker than you initially thought. As you understand that you are not at the ultimate helm of this search, you may sense a greater capacity opening. You may have learned many things about yourself that you were not expecting to learn.

At this point, you may be ready to put all of your findings together and see what emerges through the integration of these findings. Here is a key part of purpose work. You may by now have received many, seemingly conflicting messages about what you long for, what delights you and in what way you would like to make a greater contribution. But integrating this knowledge into a whole is what will lead you to your most delight-filled expression of your purpose in the world.

It's important at this point not to look at what others do. This is a time for thinking outside the box. It's also important at this point not to get attached to any one idea or outcome. Purpose is ultimately very playful, malleable, and elastic.

An interesting way of bringing this integration is to throw a "Purpose Ball" for yourself. Visualize putting all of your past selves and self-knowledge in a room together for a dance. All of you in your past experience, skills, gifts, tendencies, family gifts, as well as the people you envy or worship and whatever else you have found all get invited to mingle and dance and share time together. Allow yourself to mingle with these parts of yourself. Make it vivid! Dress the different aspects of you in beautiful costumes.

At the end of the ball, you will come away with a new friend, someone who integrates all of these parts of yourself. Your new friend will be able to tell you exactly what you are here to do. Visualize who this is. Put clothes on your friend that seem to most perfectly represent who you are, as an integrated whole. It may be that this person whispers your purpose in your ear. It may be that they give you a written note that has your purpose on it.

Sometimes the people I meet with feel that what they might be asked to do might be too big of a change from what they are doing now. But what I have seen is that the next steps are often much simpler than what is feared.

When you get all the parts of yourself in a room like this, you may find that when you integrate all that you know and have been, the next step in your purpose is right in front of you. You may find that you are already doing what this exercise suggests!

## Contemplation

One way to integrate what you have learned is to write lists of findings from all of the exercises. Write a list of the family gifts, gifts you know are yours, your skills, what part of the greater Body you are, your essence and all the other findings you have recorded or contemplated while working through this book.

Then do what I like to call a matching game. One client who did this exercise even wrote these items out on separate cards so that she could play a real matching game! You can do that or draw lines between items, making connections. Have fun with it.

Don't let the mind create traps of "impossible!" or "ridiculous!" This is an exercise to get the pathways in your brain thinking in new directions. You don't have to be running out tomorrow to do any of this!

If your mind gets too noisy in the process, take a moment to honor that voice and let it have its say, all the way to the bitter end of its argument, on a separate sheet of paper. You then can burn this "noisy" paper or make a paper airplane from it and sail it into the wastepaper basket!

# Reflections and Wonderings

# 37: Planting Intentions

Intentions are like seeds that we plant and water. We can anticipate new growth and life through creating intentions and holding them clearly in our hearts. Whether you are seeking right work, right relationships, greater abundance, creative expression, or leaving a legacy, it is beneficial to be clear about what you are intending.

Just as a seed holds the entire blueprint for a plant or tree, your intention is like the blueprint for your actions and what will arise through your actions and intention. Intention and purpose grow together, intertwined like a grafted flower. It is important to be clear about what intentions you hold. Intentions that seek the highest good for yourself and others, and that are surrendered to Divine will, ultimately will have the most satisfying outcome.

In my work with people, I often see synchronicities arise that support the path individuals have chosen through clear intention. When you create an intention for the highest good, in service of Divine will, you place yourself in the realm of Divine support. The world rises to meet you.

I've seen clients and friends receive job offers or find new love only weeks after clarifying intentions in those areas. Birds and insects or other animals often seen as messengers of Spirit pay visits that are uncanny in their timing. In my own experience, it is not unusual for people to appear out of "nowhere" to help me move forward in my next unfolding of purpose.

When we are clear on our highest intention and put it into action, it is not rare for new opportunities to arise, or for "chance" meetings to occur to help us in what we need to do next in living out our purpose.

Such synchronicities become delightful reminders of the playful, creative and often surprising ways the world of the Spirit supports us on our path. It is one of the most intriguing aspects of embracing a life of purpose.

That said, when we create intentions, it is important to be both clear as well as unattached to outcomes. Attachment to particular outcomes only leads to suffering, so going forward with clear intentions means that our hearts are clear, and our minds are open to what comes.

# Contemplation

What seeds of intention are you planting and watering? Write down your highest and best intention for your purpose in the world, your relationships, your creative pursuits, your financial picture and health. Plant these seeds by saying a prayer, asking for Divine support, or by going outdoors and speaking them to the sky or soil or trees. Your attention and care to what you have spoken is the water for your intention to grow and bear fruit. Revisit these intentions daily. Having a symbol of these intentions on your desk or posted on your refrigerator can provide a visual reminder.

# Reflections and Wonderings

# 38: Beyond Comfort

To truly follow your purpose requires guts. It requires stepping out from your comfort zone and becoming vulnerable. You must, as my morning Yogi Tea bag suggests, allow your head to bow to your heart. This is life upside down. Instead of running around protecting yourself from perceived threats, you take a chance on living your life full-out.

Why take this chance? Our inner promptings toward certain paths are the Divine Spark within us, asking us to be Divine hands and feet in the world. When we follow our purpose and live our lives with gusto, we allow ourselves to be a full expression of Divine Presence. It doesn't matter if your purpose is hauling people's garbage or working as a CEO. You can be a saint or you can be a dare devil. You can be any manifestation of Divine Essence you want to be or are called to be!

Old patterns of avoiding who we are within are addictive because they are comfortable and involve no risk. Our self-identity may even be bound up in these habits. We may feel we are a life-long critic, an "outside" observer or a discontent. The human psyche can be full of self-entrapment. To undo these traps, we must find something new that feeds us. Something that makes it worth giving up the old stories we carry around about ourselves and our world. We need something that makes us trust and lasso all of our inner resources to move forward. This is the power of purpose.

In doing the listening required to understand your purpose, you may find yourself giving up old, worn-out dreams that were based on some kind of unfulfilled desire that you no longer have. This may feel like losing a snake skin and may come with a bittersweet feeling, but if you encounter this, just know that it is one more step in the path of self-understanding.

As you unfold your purpose, you will find the truest dream is the one that moves not your ego, but the foundation of your soul.

# Contemplation

Describe your comfort zone of work or engagement with the world. Where are you, who are you relating to, what are you wearing and what time of day are you relating to people? What role are you serving?

Now imagine stretching the boundary a little to give yourself a little challenge. Stretch one or more of these arenas (the setting, the people, your role, time frame). Now describe that scenario. Imagine yourself in that scenario. The more you imagine it and feel comfortable with it, the more likely you are to develop that scenario in your world.

If you are not looking for purpose to be expressed in a particular role, but are looking for purpose in the activities you already engage in, see if you can stretch the boundary of your current scenario to provide yourself with a challenge. Challenges can grow you, and that growth itself can give you a sense of meaning and purpose!

If you are feeling as though you are surrounded by challenge but no sense of purpose, then look for small ways to engage with your world. Bake cookies and bring them to a neighbor to share. Offer to help someone with a project they find challenging. Ask someone to meet you for tea after work. It is often the smallest of gestures that can offer us the greatest meaning.

# Reflections and Wonderings

# 39: About Timing

All of the contemplation around purpose and taking risks and unfolding something new can send the message that something is currently not right about where you are. Looking at your life through this lens would be a mistake. So I just want to pause and remember how life unfolds naturally from bud to bloom.

Seen through one lens, life is perfect just the way it is. Even in the midst of immense suffering, we can raise our sights higher and see what we are learning and who we are becoming through our suffering. But seen through another lens, as we learn and grow, we can also make changes so that we bring more joy and light to our lives. As we invite more joy and light in, we have more of it to share with others.

Putting too much pressure on who and what you are becoming can create too much resistance and kickback. There is a way to hold your process as the master gardener of your own blooming. You are the one who stops to notice the exquisite nature of the bud of your own heart. And you are the master gardener who also provides water and pulls the weeds and tends the soil to nurture your own blooming.

We in the West are very goal oriented, and we are great at innovation. However, when it comes to our purpose, we cannot treat it in the same way as we would our gym schedule or project deadlines. If we put undue pressure on our own unfolding, we may set conditions that are not correct, and this may actually hinder the process.

That isn't to say you should not set goals for taking certain actions that help you explore options and ideas. These goals are part of setting conditions for your purpose to arise. The unfolding itself, however, has its own timing and its own intelligence.

The most important thing for you to do is to tend your soul, and nurture the soil of your unfolding purpose, so that you can experience the richness of the process and enjoy the blooming as it comes.

# Contemplation

Take some time to take an inventory of all that you are and all that you have been and are becoming. Express gratitude to the Divine for all that you have experienced and contain within that experience. If there is something that you are having a hard time appreciating, spend time looking at it and asking yourself if there are things that this area of your life is teaching you.

If you are experiencing emotional or physical suffering, this may be teaching you compassion. If it is lack of work, it may be teaching you a searing lesson about trust. If it is a harmful work relationship, it may be teaching you to create more clear boundaries or expressing yourself more clearly. Everything can be seen in this way. It is a way to accept your path with grace. Even if you cannot see how your current circumstances are asking you to grow, or don't feel particularly grateful for even the opportunity to grow, express gratitude anyway. Gratitude, like all positive habits of the mind and heart, can grow through practice.

# Reflections and Wonderings

# 40: Synchronicity

I've spoken about how circumstances can begin to arrange themselves to support your move toward purpose. This may happen right away or it may take a while for you to notice. In either case, it's important to keep your antennae up for these turns of event that support your process.

In the path toward understanding purpose, these serendipitous meetings, messages, signs and cues, are our confirmation that we are on the right path. Seen one way, synchronicity – the extraordinary co-arising of events that seem too lined up to be random – is the way that the universe begins to pattern itself to support our awakening of purpose. Another way to view it is that God is having fun with reminders that we are not alone and that we have someone at our back. I like both explanations and rely on both perspectives.

I have already mentioned synchronicities that I have seen individuals experience as they create clear intentions in their path toward purpose. This co-arising of life is dynamic, playful, and even downright unnerving at times! But it is in support our highest unfolding. Following are additional examples.

A client who is a leader in a non-profit organization, who has just resigned from her job is immediately approached by an organization close to her heart about taking on consulting work. An artist who has just narrowed her purpose to arts administration and education out of the blue gets an email about a local job opening in just that field. Looking to embrace her own power more, a client is suddenly presented with a situation that requires her to step into a leadership role before a large audience.

Such synchronicity increases our faith that our path is deeply guided and supported here. We are each a dynamic aspect of a much greater Dynamism that is elastic and synchronized with our highest intentions, aspirations and soul evolution.

As we enter this fluid aspect of following purpose, life becomes more magical, more of a mystery tour, more of a theatrical play whose script is written on our very own hearts.

# Contemplation

Keep note of any synchronicities that may appear and what they say to you. What they say to you is more important than what appears. It may be a chance meeting related to the area you were exploring. It may be that you keep hearing the same message or seeing the same billboard that speaks to something you are already sensing. It may be a note from a friend. It may be a vivid nighttime dream that is an answer a question you were posing.

Watching for such signs takes discernment. Signs may simply be possibilities presenting themselves to you. How you interpret the signs has more to do with the trajectory of your purpose than the signs themselves. A trusted friend or mentor can be a helpful mirror in discussing such synchronicities and teasing out possible meanings.

# Reflections and Wonderings

# 41: Mini Purposes

As you integrate the knowledge of who you are and who you are becoming, there is a way for your purpose to have immediate direction and grounding. This is through the function of mini-purposes.

A friend of mine came up with the idea of mini-purposes while we were taking an exercise walk in our local park. We regularly walk and talk about our steps toward our big picture vision for our lives, to help keep each other on track. "Mini-purposes" are related to these steps, but unlike steps with a larger endgame in mind, they are self-contained purposes. They *are* the goal!

It is easy to miss the beauty of the day because we are focused on the to—do list or the future goals, dreams or desires. The idea of mini-purposes is to help us bring attention to what is unfolding now, today, right now.

So if the goal is to make some connections in the field you are interested in pursuing, the purpose of the day is to make those connections, but make them with heart and soul. The purpose may be to "make inspiring connections." When you create that as a purpose, you set out with an intention to create meaning in those connections. What you do in each step is purposeful and meaningful. You may even find that you make connections beyond what you expected!

We all know the ramifications of work that is done hurriedly and without thought. We have either experienced how it feels to do such work, or how it feels to be at the receiving end of such work. Mini-purposes create thought around each activity that you do.

Mini-purposes can be created for a particular task, for an hour, a day, a week, a year. You can use min-purposes in helping you bring your purpose to the world in the most purposeful way! Or if you feel that your own purpose is not unfolding fast enough for your comfort level, mini-purposes can help bring fulfillment to the moments at hand.

# Contemplation

Think of something that you would like to bring a sense of purpose to. It may be how you relate to a particular colleague, or a plan to explore a certain line of work. It may be certain tasks that you need to do but have a hard time getting to or find unpleasant.

Create a mini-purpose for this area of your life for today. What do you want to experience, and how do you want to experience it? You can map out mini-purposes for as many things as you feel would be useful.

You may want to write the purpose out and post it somewhere so that you can see it. This will help bring your attention back to purpose if it strays.

# Reflections and Wonderings

# 42: What's in Your Teacup?

Here's a personal story about integrating purpose into daily life.

There was a day this past year that I had had it with how my work was going. I was putting a lot of effort into administrative tasks and wanted to be doing the more creative things like writing. I was not managing my time well. The whole thing felt *wrong.*

My husband Jonathan is a good listener so he listened patiently as I listed all of the things that I saw as simply unworkable. It was a litany of complaint, most of them coming from simply feeling tired that day.

When I was done, Jonathan sat for a little while, and then said, with simple compassion, "That is your cup to drink."

I was startled by this response. It shook me all the way to the root of my being. I was not expecting that response. And he was so right. There was nowhere to go with these complaints. There was nothing to fix, nothing to undo. There was the simple knowledge that this was my cup.

"You know," he continued, sparingly, "I have my own cup. We all have our cup to drink."

Often the quickest path out of our internal suffering is acceptance. When we resist what is in our cup, we create a lot of unnecessary noise.

We all have our cup to drink. Some days, we may feel as though this cup is way too full of tiring material. On other days, we may be giddily drinking the elixir of the gods. But every day, we have a cup. And it is our very own cup. As we drink this cup, we can know ourselves and know life better for the drinking of it.

Sometimes we have to accept things that seem unacceptable, even heart breaking. Yet from this very acceptance comes an abundance of spirit and heart. It is out of this acceptance that we can embrace our unfolding purpose in all its complexity. Even when we don't feel it is so, we hold a blessed cup belonging to a blessed life.

# Contemplation

Write down every single thing that is in your cup today. You may even draw a picture of a teacup in your journal, and write these things in it. Write down all of the things that you hold as worries, fears and concerns. Write down everything that you can think of that you are holding as burdens. Then write down all of the things that bring you joy. Next, write down all of the new qualities and external manifestations of these qualities that you would like to invite into your life.

Express gratitude for all of these things, for both what is present now and what you are opening your heart to experiencing. All of it makes up your blessed cup today.

# Reflections and Wonderings

# 43: Trust: A Dragonfly Story

Understanding purpose is an exercise in trust. We must trust that what we need will arise to support our path. We must trust that if we make significant changes in our lives to move closer to our purpose, that those changes will be worth the effort. We must trust that we will find purpose and be given the strength to follow it.

This story was inspired by a conversation with a friend of mine:

"Trust!" the dragonfly said, doing a little dance and fluttering its wings.

The man, sitting by the lake, looked at the dragonfly and said, "I'm not so sure."

"Trust!" the dragonfly said, flying in two loops and then standing on its head.

The man looked at the dragonfly and said, "Trust in whom?"

"Trust!" the dragonfly said, buzzing over the man's head and then landing on his ear.

The man pondered this for a while, and then said, "What if I end up with nothing?"

The dragonfly giggled a little, which meant that its wings buzzed, tickling the man's ear.

"What is nothing?" the dragonfly whispered, just loud enough for the man to hear.

"Nothing is when you lose everything and you are poor and destitute and you feel that no one will ever love you again."

The dragonfly considered this for a while. It scratched its little dragonfly head with a dragonfly foot. Its nature was so different than that of men. It seemed that the world of human beings was full of this kind of thinking and questioning. For the dragonfly, it was not its nature to question. But because the dragonfly loved the man with all of its dragonfly essence, it considered this question for a long, long time.

When evening set in, and the sky was turning colors of purple and orange and pink, the dragonfly found the answer. The dragonfly did a little dance in front of the man, signaling him to pay attention. Then the dragonfly headed straight toward the sun. As it flew, a little trail of silver followed its path. It was not a straight path but was looping and had a rhythm all its own. When the dragonfly got to the sun, the sun and the dragonfly disappeared down below the horizon, leaving only a purple hue.

The man, who watched the whole dance, noticed that the color of the sky was the color of the dragonfly. It was tender, the man thought, seeing how the dragonfly would go to such ends to answer his question.

But he wondered what it meant. Why would the dragonfly disappear like that? He went home, puzzled.

The next day, the dragonfly was sitting on a log near the lake, when the man approached.

"I thought you were gone," the man said to the little dragon-winged creature.

"Trust," the dragonfly said, and did a little dance, fluttering its wings.

## Contemplation

In what or whom do you place your trust? Is it God, Allah, Siva, the angels, a guru, a teacher? Write down the one in whom you have a sense of trust, no matter how faint. Just the act of this naming can be an exercise in trust! You may find yourself writing down many names!

Now name an area that you feel doubtful about. You might want to name several areas. Visualize placing those situations in the hands of the one whom you named. Watch these doubts being taken from you, like packages being lifted from your hands or shoulders. Release control of these areas. Ask that these doubts be replaced with the lighter quality of trust.

# Reflections and Wonderings

# 44: Follow the Prompting

As a coach, I work with a lot of people who have overridden the voice of their hearts, that still quiet inner prompting that guides us on our way. Many people do not trust this inner voice.

To rediscover this voice takes time. It took me years, and I'm still learning. But with practice and patience, the voice of the mind will lie down and the quieter, heart-led voice will emerge.

On the path toward purpose, this inner prompting is the most valuable tool that we have. And the practice is easy: the more we follow the prompts, the more we hear them, and the more we receive feedback that helps guide us in following these prompts in the future.

To help people develop this inner listening skill, I often suggest that they follow simple prompts. Not the prompt, *quit your job tomorrow,* but maybe: *go ahead and make that call to a former colleague.*

Here is a story about following the inner prompts, and how the outcomes are not always what we expect.

One day last year, I followed an inner prompting to follow a rainbow. It was a full rainbow, treetop to treetop, and I wanted to get a good picture of it. So I drove to the next town over, aptly named Plainsboro as it has flat farmlands and plains. However, once I got to Plainsboro, the rainbow was already gone.

Still, I felt led. I was only a quarter mile from a Vedic Studies center that I'd wanted to visit for years. I decided to finally stop in. When I knocked on the door, an Indian man with a humble demeanor greeted me at the door. I shook his hand, asking about who I could talk to about the center. He led me to a man seated at a table not far from a prayer room.

As I talked to this gentleman, whose name was David, and learned that the man I'd just met was Swami Shantananda, a teacher that some (including David) consider their guru. I felt honored and humbled in meeting this unassuming Swami, who had just shook my hand without introduction.

The Swami was hovering nearby, and so we exchanged a few words before he retired to his quarters. I was delighted. A guru, right around the corner. It brightened my day more than the rainbow did. When I told the story to a friend of mine, she said: "You found the rainbow, only the rainbow was in the form of a Swami!"

One of the interesting developments from that rainbow chasing was that David, I learned through our conversation, works as a professional photographer. I took his card, and we stayed in touch. He took my photograph for this book.

Acting on inner prompting can sometimes make us feel like we are losing our minds. And we are! We are losing the gripping of the mind, so that the heart can have its say. You never know where this kind of listening will lead you. It is a mystical tour, a journey of the heart.

## Contemplation

Describe the last three times you listened to inner promptings and what the outcome was. Was it what you expected? If not, was the outcome useful in some way?

Take some time right now to listen. Put your awareness in your heart or solar plexus and ask a specific question. The first answer is often the one that is most true. But listen for a while, and see what arises. Commit to following this prompting, without attachment to the outcome.

The next time you feel an urge to do something or say something, see what happens next. Do you automatically tamp it down and ignore it? If so, follow the prompt instead. Don't be attached to the outcome. Just follow as a practice in listening.

If you are really serious about developing your listening, keep a listening journal. Write down what the prompts are, how you follow the prompts and what the outcomes are.

Begin to ask your heart: *Show me how to bring my purpose into the world.* Then listen for the prompts!

# Reflections and Wonderings

# 45: Releasing Doubt

We've been talking about how purpose unfolds. Barring a sudden event that calls out your purpose, purpose unfolds most gracefully from an inner quality of spaciousness. The difficulty of inner listening is that the mind can find so many ways of keeping that space filled with doubt.

The mind can be our best ally, or it can be the most fearsome saboteur of our purpose. Gaining a measure of control over the mind's mayhem is a benefit of meditation and mindfulness tools.

One of the tools that can be most effective is using the breath for releasing negative thinking and doubt. One deep, cleansing breath can be like a reviving inner waterfall, washing away habitual thoughts. Although its benefits may only be momentary, use of the breath in this way over time can re-pattern the brain to stop its habitual mental path and allow for the new territory of your purpose to evolve.

Take three deep belly breaths right now and listen to the sound. All of your power of focus goes into listening for the breath. In that focus, any over-thinking or negative thinking that may want to dominate just doesn't have a place to go. (If it does, take louder or longer breaths!)

The sound of the breath is soothing to the ear. In that sound, the mind can rest from its weary pursuit of problem-solving, seeking, judging or whatever it is your mind tends to do.

Focusing on the sound of the breath as it enters and exits your body is a time-honored meditation practice. However, it is not something you have to close your eyes to do. You can do it when you are at your desk, or when you are driving. You can do it when you are on the train, or shoveling snow. The great thing about the breath is that it is always with you. It is a portable tool. When you are worried, or you are driving yourself crazy with thought, wherever you are, remember, peace exists right now, in this moment, in this breath!

Breathe, and let the mind take a breath. Use this beautiful, God-given tool to cleanse the body and mind of harmful thought patterns and leave open a space for something new to arise.

# Contemplation

Here is an exercise to use the breath and intention to let the mind take a break.

Write down everything that is bothering you. Just get it all out!

Write down the name of every person with whom you have conflicts or about whom you have concerns.

Write down all the reasons that you cannot follow your purpose right now or create meaning in the way that you want to.

Now close your eyes and breathe. Let go of this list on the sound of your breath. Breathe all of these things out on the out breath. Breathe in peace on the in breath. Give this list to Divine Reality to manage. Ask that this list be managed by Divine Reality, so that you can let it go. Ask to be shown ways of being and doing and thinking that serve your highest calling.

# Reflections and Wonderings

# 46: A Hidden Passion

Sometimes a passion has to go underground before it is reborn. We may be passionate about something at age six that we don't rediscover until age forty-three. We may have entered a profession early on that we were passionate about only to get off track and lose touch with that passion. We may have known we were passionate about something our entire lives but never gave ourselves permission to express it in the world.

Just as the bulbs that stay underground in winter give birth to new life in the spring, so it can be with what we long to express. I believe this is a necessary part of how we unfold as humans. We cannot express all parts of ourselves at once. Some parts must remain hidden.

Sometimes, a passion can go underground for years. A person may not even realize that it is there until it emerges like a surprise. The key part of reigniting this passion is patience as you rediscover what seems lost.

The truth is that nothing is ever lost. It is just remade. We are beings that unfold, and we can't unfold all aspects of ourselves at once. Perhaps in one season of our lives, we unfold the artist. At another time, the mother. At yet another time, the business woman. Perhaps we even unfold an aspect of the child and begin to discover the world as if for the first time.

If you have a passion that feels hidden, whether it has ever seen the light of day or not, you may feel that expressing that passion now may be next to impossible. It may feel out of reach.

If this is the case, some investigation of your expectations could be very useful. If you wanted to be a star athlete, for example, you may now feel defeatist if you have missed the age window to attain this goal. However, the impulse to excel physically may be the very passion that is needed now to awaken you and your life and lend you a sense of purpose.

More often than not, it is the pleasure of pushing the limits of our own expression that is more filling to the soul than any kind of "endgame" associated with this expression. Expression has its own unique rewards.

Passion is always with us. It may not always feel present, but it is the quality of our life force that is dynamic and urges us to take on life's challenges with gusto. Passion drives us to embrace life, despite everything.

# Contemplation

If you have a passion that is hiding out, make note of that in your journal. It may be something simple such as a fun pastime or it may be more complex than that, such as a former line of work or career pursuit. Write down all of the ways that this passion was expressed in the past, and how it felt for you to express this passion. Now chronicle the ways that this passion is expressed in different areas of your life. It may be through relationships, a new creative pursuit or hobby or creative aspects of your work that draw on the same inner passion.

Ask yourself if you would like to reawaken this passion in a particular form, and ask yourself if you are ready (two different questions). If the answer is yes to both of those questions, write down one concrete step that you can take to bring this expression back into your daily life. Commit to taking that step by a certain date/time that you mark on your calendar.

If you answered that you would like to revive this passion but aren't ready, write down all of the conditions that you need to have met so that it feels like the right time to start. Commit to creating at least one of those conditions by a certain date or time, and mark this on your calendar.

# Reflections and Wonderings

# 47: Holy Thou

I want to take a moment to talk about relationships, because our purpose unfolds in the context of a web of relationships. Many of the people who come to see me about purpose also want to talk about purposeful relationships. I will share a helpful lens here to help you create dynamic, exciting relationships that can weather the challenges life brings your way and support your creation of a meaningful and purposeful life.

Earlier, I mentioned caring for the body as a temple for the Spirit. To consider myself a temple, I must see that others around me are also this temple. I'm not the only temple in town, in other words! In this way, I not only foster the flourishing of my own life, but I foster its flourishing all around me. I help create a context in which grace and purpose and meaning can arise through these everyday interactions.

Instead of seeing an annoying line in front of me at the store, I practice seeing a row of holy temples, true houses for the Spirit. Instead of focusing on the failings of friends or family, I practice seeing a living, breathing temple of Spirit. Instead of seeing the world for its failings, I practice seeing that the planet is populated by billions of mini-temples of light. It's not an easy practice, but what you practice eventually becomes the reality you walk around in.

It is very easy to see what is not working in your relationships, your health, your financial picture, your world, etc. It is easy to find enemies and to build internal walls for self-protection. But if you view yourself and others as temples of light, a much different picture emerges.

If I consider you as a holy place, then I see not so much of the ways that you fail, but the ways that you operate as a holy being. Even if you do not choose to see yourself as a holy being, I can see you as this. I can see how even your shadow side teaches me about life and our contradictions. And even if you fail horribly, I see the way that you are still holy. You are still the embodiment of a much greater soul that is connected to the Soul of eternity. If I look for this, even amid calamity, I can find it.

I practice this with my husband, when we have a conflict. I remember that he is a holy being, and that he deserves my utmost respect and honor. I also practice this with my son when we are at odds. I remember that he is a holy teacher, reminding me to speak more gently, walk more gently, and listen more keenly. I also practice this with friends and family, when my own insecurities arise and I look for somewhere to place blame. I am surrounded by holiness and reminders to look within to find places where shifts need to occur.

This practice is not meant to create passivity but rather personal responsibility. It is a way of looking at the world that invites a deeper sense of peace and understanding of the human condition. We are all Divine Spark, housed in beautiful, frail, temporary houses. When we honor each other as holy beings, it eases mental anguish and creates space for a much greater awareness. Deeper meaning grows out from this awareness.

## Contemplation

Take a moment to see yourself through the eyes of the Beloved. Write a note to yourself from this perspective. What would the Divine see in you that you are not seeing? What would the Divine tell you about following your delight? What would this Presence tell you about following your purpose? Write a long letter to yourself as though from the Divine, telling you about your path.

Think of someone you love, and write a note to this person, from this same deeper perspective. You can even think of someone you are having a hard time with, and write a note to this person. What would the Beloved see in that person that you are not seeing? You do not need to send the notes. Just write them so that you can see with fresh perspective.

# Reflections and Wonderings

# 48: The Illusion of the Future

It is a human tendency, at least in the West, to pin our hopes, dreams and aspirations onto one single achievement in the future. When we at last "arrive" at our destination, whether it is a degree or a job or an award, we expect big changes and some sense of having "arrived." However, in reality, when we get there, we find that we are the same person as we were before. Nothing has truly changed. We find the illusion of our projection.

Like Dorothy in the *Wizard of Oz*, we find that the wizard behind the veil is just a plain, ordinary human being with no special power. Our destination, instead of containing the power we thought it would contain, is simply empty of magic and is ordinary.

It is tempting to project all sorts of things onto finding purpose. It is true that living your purpose can give you direction and meaning; it can give you a reason to get out of bed in the morning. However, purpose is not an endgame. Purpose may help you channel your energies in the right direction, but you still have to address the challenges that come along the way.

It is easy to imagine that once you have found your purpose in the world, life will be easier, and you will stop struggling. This is simply a false ideal. In fact, when you have found your purpose, you may struggle even more! You may find that your resistance to following this purpose that was once at twenty percent is now at eighty percent!

The great news about illusion is that it compels us on our path toward understanding. When we "arrive" and feel the emptiness of our arrival, we can see what life is truly made of. Like Dorothy in her ruby slippers, we can exclaim, "There's no place like home!" There is no place like the home of the heart, the home of union with the Presence within.

I meet with people who work hard at living out their purpose and who grapple with ever new and interesting challenges both internal and external. In starting out with this awareness, you can work toward living your purpose with eyes wide open, embracing every step of the way.

Purpose is an unveiled truth. Understanding your purpose is about embracing who you are and what you are about without the illusion of what future this purpose might bring.

# Contemplation

Give some thought to what you expect when you find your purpose. Here is a game to help:

Imagine that you have just found your purpose written in a fortune cookie. There it is, in tiny red print, accompanied perhaps by some lucky numbers and a Chinese word and its meaning. How do you feel, now that you know? What is happening to your breath? Are you more relaxed? Now, what images are in your mind? Those are projections.

Now bring yourself back to the present. How do you feel now?

Jump back and forth between who you are now and who you are with your purpose. See if you can stabilize the feeling of having purpose in your body. This is designed to break through any illusion of you being separate from what you project into the future.

When you accept that these are the same, then there is no need to project anything onto your purpose. You can simply let it unfold from the present, through the mindful activities and mini-purposes that you engage in.

# Reflections and Wonderings

# 49: The Passion Within

Your heart, when open and listening and ready to merge with Divine Purpose, is in the throes of awakening passion. Passion is a life force that unifies our own gifts and willingness to contribute to the world with a much larger Divine Presence operating through us. Surrendering to the knowledge that we are this place of unification of the finite with Infinite Intelligence and Love is potent, healing and reviving to the soul.

When you combine this passion with purpose you become a potent and unifying force in the world. As with the mountain stream, you may experience the flow of the Divine Beloved through everything that you do. Even when you encounter obstacles, you may find that you can work with them more quickly, because you are motivated to carrying out your purpose with grace. Your work becomes a fulfillment of a greater Work, whose impact in the lives of others you will never fully know.

One of the ways that I keep in tune with this inner passion is to occasionally sit with my eyes closed and visualize the entire planet. In this visualization, the planet resides in the space of my heart. All of the people, creatures, vegetation, rock formations, lava, air, oceans, reside in that tiny space, all together.

Yet as I'm aware of this planet in the space of my heart, I'm also aware of how my heart is much bigger than my body. My heart, when I open to it, is unified with the Divine Heart. And so in my awareness, I expand beyond my physical form and into eternity, and I can see how all of life is held in this Greater, Loving Heart.

We are so much more than we are aware of! We are so tiny yet so expansive. We are so full of complaints and yet so blessed. Our truest passion resides in this place of perhaps not understanding but simply embracing the All that resides within, and how we reside in the All.

Your Divine Purpose is being born from an impossible union of what we think of as opposites: infinite and finite. No wonder it can get us tied up in knots! And yet, relaxing into this knowledge, we can let go of a sense of controlling the outcome. We can know that all we need to do is listen and follow the prompts of a greater Passion.

# Contemplation

Visualize the planet, as in the meditation just mentioned. If that feels too immense, visualize one person who has a place in your heart.

Recognize, in this visualization how the place of the heart is not fixed in time or space.

Next, imagine all of the people that you want to serve in the place of your heart. If it is animals or plants or geological formations you want to serve, then visualize these! Let your heart connect to these beings through a beam of light or simply just sensing that connection.

Make a commitment to serve these beings through your highest capacity.

# Reflections and Wonderings

# 50: Anchoring Your Purpose

Once you have a sense of your purpose, you have a working template for further action and ways of being in your life. Your purpose will evolve and change over time, but now is the time to embrace what you have gathered so far. Now is the time to anchor this awareness in your daily life, so that you can experience its power each and every day.

There are several ways that I suggest anchoring your purpose into your awareness and your life. The first is to simply name it and frame it! Write down your purpose, as you understand it, and post it somewhere as a reminder that this is the framework for your life from this point onward. Sharing this purpose with friends and family can help create support for living out your purpose.

If you are looking at a big change such as setting up your own business, taking on a major project or quitting your job, engaging a set of friends or a mentor to support you in this process can help you stay on track. You can navigate this process by using "mini-purposes" as discussed earlier in this book.

A third way to anchor purpose is through creating a visual reminder. I've always found it helpful to have a bulletin board above my writing desk, with symbols of inspiration and purpose. Images can be very powerful daily reminders of our conscious expression of purpose.

Another way to anchor purpose is to do vision work. What I mean by this is spending time, either alone or with a key person or group of people in your life, in meditation and contemplation. In this meditation, you can ask for the most authentic expression of your purpose in the world or you can ask about next steps. You can use the exercise from the "Imagine" contemplation that appears earlier in this book or create one of your own.

The benefit of doing this work with another person or in a group is that there may be similarities in what each of you discover in this inward asking. It can be very helpful and confirming to have these similarities, as it is an indication that you have tapped into the same stream of knowledge. You may also receive helpful feedback in further refining what you have found.

You may want to start a new purpose journal, to take note of how your purpose asks you to live and be in the world on a daily basis. You may want to record actions that you are taking, goals that you are setting and meeting, people you are meeting or dreams that you are living.

If you find yourself resisting putting your purpose into words or an image, or resisting doing anything to anchor your purpose, ask yourself why. Often, when people get to this stage, they begin to fear their own power or fear failure or encounter other kinds of fears. If this sounds accurate to you, acknowledge this fear. This is resistance making sure that you are going forward mindfully and taking care of the ego self that wants to feel secure. Acknowledge this fear, and then let go of it, and find a way to anchor your purpose that brings it powerfully to your consciousness every day.

However you choose to anchor your purpose in your life, you can be assured that it will continue to unfold and provide opportunities for you to live it out every day. Keeping your purpose at the forefront of your awareness will help you meet challenges that arise with a greater sense of grace and help keep you focused on living out this purpose every day.

## Contemplation

Anchor your purpose this week through an external action. You can choose one of the ways described above, or create your own way. Choose at least one person in your life and share this purpose with this person. Don't worry about what this person may think. Instead, consider how he or she might be inspired! If you need a way in to that conversation, share this book with this person and use it as a talking point.

# Reflections and Wonderings

# 51: Be Who You Are

One morning last spring I took a walk around my suburban neighborhood, contemplating how powerful it is to have a sense of your soul's purpose. Whether that purpose is to organize or to build, to write or to tend—or any of the limitless purposes we can imagine—how powerful to stand in your purpose and know that this is why you are on the planet!

Then I came upon a green patch of grass highlighted with the small but sunny pom-pom offerings of dandelion flowers. I love dandelions. I was blessed with two Pennsylvania German grandmothers, both of whom made a delicious dandelion salad. To me, dandelions are a healing and nutritious herb, not a weed.

What popped into my head as I walked by these dandelions was: what if the dandelion wanted to be a tulip? How sad that dandelion would be! It would try and try, and the fire of this kind of mental anguish would make it droopy and sad. Maybe it would wilt and die before its time. And in the end, it would still be a dandelion, just a sad one.

Thank God dandelions just embrace who they are. They stand powerfully in their dandelion suits and shine yellow and puffy for all to see. At some point, they change form and turn into a translucent globe of seeds—a ball of pure potential! Lucky for us (and Pennsylvania German grandmothers) these seeds blow and take root and populate the earth with new life and growth.

And this is how it is when we use our power to choose to express our own gifts and our own purpose and stand powerfully in that expression. When we do this, we become beautiful manifestations of Divine Love in human form. Even more, we become translucent globes of possibility, and the seeds of our actions take root and grow in ways we can hardly imagine.

# *Contemplation*

Take some time to contemplate who you are. What defines you? Is it all that is in your cup for that day? Do those things define you? If I were to say your purpose is to be you, who would that be?

Here is an exercise to sink down into your body and find an awareness of *you*. Sit with your eyes closed and put your awareness in your abdomen, which is the seat of intuitive knowledge. Who are you? You may find that you are a bright vessel. You may find that you are something more solid. You may find that you are undefined. Whatever you find, embrace this human experience that you find yourself in, at this moment. The world is longing for an authentic expression of your deepest being. Be who you are.

# Reflections and Wonderings

# 52: Enjoy the Creative Process

We are planted in an exquisite garden of love and shadow that transcends personal experience. Why we are planted here as a human race, I cannot say! But why you are here, personally, I imagine you have a better idea of now that you are at the end of this book.

We live in a universe that is highly creative. When you set out to find your purpose, you set in motion a whole realm of unseen support to guide you in this process. You begin to re-pattern the very fabric of your life from this most deeply-held impulse.

I don't believe in chance. I believe that we are coursing toward the center of our beings, all together, collectively finding that place where Spirit and matter do not exist separately but are a dynamic and exciting play of creation. As we take this journey together, we change the fabric of our lives, we change the fabric of society, we change the fabric of life itself. And as we surrender to the reality of this process, we are deeply and magnificently changed.

I want to say here: don't stop believing, and asking, and probing and becoming. Allow all that you have learned to gestate and then act on what you have learned. I meet too many people who have let their inner life whither or let their bold dreams die, and I wonder *why?* Let the Divine move you and change you and open you and then maybe even take you out of your comfortable garden and replant you somewhere else so that you have more room to grow!

If you don't act on behalf of yourself, then act on behalf of those around you. Act on behalf of the planet. Because the planet really needs you. Yes, the planet really needs YOU to do what your soul requires and to be all that you are already, deep down. The planet needs the most authentic Beloved YOU!

I'm so honored to be planted in this magnificent garden with you, in this period of rapid evolution of human consciousness. May you live fully the Divine Purpose that is unfolding in you right now. May you deepen into that place where you can feel that Divine Spark and inner passion igniting you and your life. May you live freely and peacefully and bloom and grow, remembering who you are and why you are here.

# Contemplation

Take some time to reflect on your purpose as an answer to the question, "Why am I here?" Does it fully answer this question, or is something more needed? Tweak your purpose to include anything else that you feel is important in answering this fundamental question. Your purpose may be a word, a sentence, or it may be an entire paragraph. It is possible that you may have a clear sense of it but be unable to describe it in language. Perhaps you might try drawing it, or simply holding the awareness of it in your heart. However you hold your purpose, it is fully and utterly an expression of who you are and what you have come here to do. It is yours to be blessed by and yours with which to bless others.

Thank you for participating in this journey. I thank you for being who you are and being willing to ask the big questions. Now, it is time to be the answer.

# Reflections and Wonderings

# About the Author

Cynthia Yoder guides people in making powerful and purposeful choices in their work and relationships and helps them in overcoming the inevitable road blocks along the way. She has worked with artists, writers, CEOs, small business owners and other professionals in their quest to make meaningful and significant contributions to the communities they serve.

Cynthia's unique approach combines her practical understanding of traditional work environments with six years of study with spiritual teacher and author David La Chapelle, where she learned the application of meditation, visualization, sound healing and intuitive listening to help others follow their purpose and attain greater meaning in their lives.

Her work with leaders stems from ten years of public relations work where she learned from and promoted inspiring world leaders. As a freelance writer for Princeton University and Bristol Myers-Squibb, she interviewed and wrote articles about leaders in art, politics and science including Paul Muldoon and Joy Behar. As the communications director at New York's Cathedral of St. John the Divine, Cynthia promoted events for Hillary Clinton, the Dalai Lama, Al Gore, Diana Ross and many other world leaders and artists. Her work as a coach began in 2000, when she lassoed these experiences to offer public relations coaching for artists and small businesses.

Cynthia's own search for purpose began in her twenties, leading to the publication of her spiritual memoir, *Crazy Quilt: Pieces of a Mennonite Life.* She has given inspirational readings and talks at Princeton University, Yale School of Divinity, the American Association of University Women, Barnes and Nobles Bookstores and many other forums.

Cynthia studied on the graduate level at Columbia University, receiving her MFA in Writing from Sarah Lawrence College. Cynthia's writings have appeared in *New Jersey Monthly, Mothering, Tiferet* and are included in an upcoming Barclay Press anthology of mothers raising their children to understand peace, justice and simplicity.

She lives in New Jersey with her husband Jonathan and son Gabriel.

*To receive ongoing support and inspiration for your path, subscribe to Cynthia's newsletter or read her blog on www.cynthiayoder.com.*

# About the Artwork and Artist

The art on the cover of this book is a detail of *Clyde's Emerson*, a seven-foot high interactive sculpture by artist Jerry Wennstrom. Jerry's early search for purpose is a fascinating one and worth mentioning. In 1979, Jerry was a rising star in the New York art world when he let go of his identity as an artist by intentionally destroying his large body of art and giving away his possessions. With this leap of faith Jerry embarked on a decade of wandering, listening, seeking and relying on intuition and unconditional trust to guide and provide for him. His inspiring story is documented in The Parabola/Sentient Publications documentary film, *In The Hands of Alchemy*, and Jerry's own book, *The Inspired Heart*.

Today, Jerry continues to create art and write. He travels internationally, offering film presentations as well as inspirational lectures and workshops. His new body of art is showcased in the recently released film, *Mythic Journeys* by Steve and Whitney Boe. He is currently consulting with award-winning Danish filmmaker Hans Fabian Wullenweber, who is making a feature-length film based on Jerry's life story.

Jerry's current works are thought-provoking and often whimsical commentaries on human experience. You can view some of these works on www.handsofalchemy.com. *Clyde's Emerson* consists of a 1950s' TV (housing a zoetrope with images changing from death to life), carved cedar images, mechanical devices, a variety of brass and copper components and other found and created items.

Breinigsville, PA USA
30 November 2010
250286BV00003B/37-108/P